About GIMP

GIMP (GNU Image Manipulation Program) is a free multi-platform photo manipulation tool. The GIMP is suitable for a variety of image manipulation tasks, including photo retouching, image composition, and image ~~~~~~~~~~. It works on the following platforms: GNU/Linux™, Apple M~~~~~~~~~~~~ft Windows™, OpenBSD™, NetBSD™, FreeBSD™ ~~~~~~~~~~~~~~~ HP-UX™, Tru64™, Digital UNIX™, OSF/1™, ~~~~~~

The GIMP is a Free ~~~~~~~~~~~~~~~~~~~~neral Public License [GPL]. The GPL provides ~~~~~~~~~~~~~~~~~~~~alter the source code that makes up computer ~~~~

Brighter Days with GIMP

This book Covers GIMP from start to finish.

Chapter 1. Introduction
Chapter 2. Fire up the GIMP
Chapter 3. First Steps with Wilber
Chapter 4. Getting Unstuck
Chapter 5. Getting Images into GIMP
Chapter 6. Getting Images out of GIMP
Chapter 7. Painting with GIMP
Chapter 8. Combining Images
Chapter 9. Text Management
Chapter 10. Enhancing Photographs
Chapter 11. Color Management with GIMP
Chapter 12. Enrich my GIMP
Chapter 13. Scripting

Plus a bonus section

Part III: Detailed Function Reference.
Part III (three) explains function Reference in a detailed form with fully colored images, its chapters includes: **Chapter14: Tools, Chapter 15: Dialogs, Chapter 16: Menus and Chapter 17: Filters.** The above listed chapters have sections and sub sections.
A great way of knowing more about GIMP 2.8.

Brighter Days with GIMP

The A-Z GIMP User Guide.

By

U. C-Abel Books.

Legal Notice

All Rights Reserved

First Edition: 2015

Copyright @ U. C-Abel Books. ISBN-13: 978-1517337179

This book, **Brighter Days with GIMP** with ISBN-13: 978-1517337179 has been licensed by copyright proprietors, therefore reproducing it in whatever way without a prior written permission from the copyright holder is an infringement of copyright and violators will be punished.

However, some parts of this book is freely available at www.gimp.org. Visit the website if you want it for any purpose but be sure to read their legal documentation and for peace sake, don't copy from this book.

ISBN-13: 978-1517337179

ISBN-10: 1517337178

Published by U. C-Abel Books

Introduction

GIMP (GNU Image Manipulation Program) is a free multi-platform photo manipulation tool. The GIMP is suitable for a variety of image manipulation tasks, including photo retouching, image composition, and image construction. It works on the following platforms: GNU/Linux™, Apple Mac OS X™, Microsoft Windows™, OpenBSD™, NetBSD™, FreeBSD™, Solaris™, SunOS™, AIX™, HP-UX™, Tru64™, Digital UNIX™, OSF/1™, IRIX™, OS/2™, and BeOS™.

The GIMP is a Free Software application covered by the General Public License [GPL]. The GPL provides users with the freedom to access and alter the source code that makes up computer programs.

In sincerity, we never thought of selling this book or bringing it to the public at first, we only compiled it to help ourselves use this image manipulation program called GIMP better, and as well have something we can run to when a challenge shows up.

The main cause for this publication is to help Independent Authors and Publishers whom we often see their post consigning their books' interior or cover on most writers forums asking how to do this or that, or even the program to use for them; when you reason alongside with us, you will know that Indies need genuine help; another category of people we have in mind is designers who want to know more about the program they use in order not be found unfamiliar with any part. This book is for users of GIMP of any level (Beginner, Medium or Expert) and for any profession: Designers, Photographers, Illustrators, Artists or any other category so far as image manipulation with GIMP is concerned.

Get in love with GIMP, manipulate your image in whatsoever manner that seems good to you.

Happy GIMPing!

Table of Contents

Legal Notice i
Introduction ii
Table of Content iii

Part 1 — Getting Started

Chapter 1: Introduction 1
   1. Welcome to GIMP 1
      1.1. Authors 1
      1.2. The GIMP Help system 1
      1.3. Features and Capabilities 2
   2. What's New in GIMP 2.8? 2

Chapter 2: Fire up the GIMP 13
   1. Running GIMP 13
   2. 1.1. Known Platforms 13
   3. 1.2. Language 13
   4. 1.3. Command Line Arguments 14
   5. 2. Starting GIMP the first time 17
   6. 2.1. Finally 17

Chapter 3: First Steps with Wilber 18
   1. Basic Concepts 18
   2. Main Windows 22
      2.1. The Toolbox 25
      2.2. Image Window 27
      2.3. Dialogs and Docking 31
   3. Undoing 36
      3.1. Things That Cannot be Undone 37
   4. Common Tasks 38
      4.1. Intention 38
      4.2. Change the Size of an Image for the screen 39
      4.3. Change the Size of an Image for print 41
      4.4. Compressing Images 42
      4.5. Crop An Image 45
      4.6. Find Info About Your Image 48
      4.7. Change the Mode 49
      4.8. Flip An Image 52
      4.9. Rotate An Image 54
      4.10. Separating an Object From Its Background 55

5. How to Draw Straight Lines 59
    5.1. Intention 60
    5.2. Examples 63

Chapter 4: Getting Unstuck 65
1. Getting Unstuck 65
    1.1. Stuck! 65
    1.2. Common Causes of GIMP Non-Responsiveness 65

Part II — How do I Become a GIMP Wizard?

Chapter 5: Getting Images into GIMP 72
1. Image Types 72
2. Creating new Files 75
3. Opening Files 75
    3.1. Open File 75
    3.2. Open Location 77
    3.3. Open Recent 78
    3.4. Using External Programs 78
    3.5. File Manager 78
    3.6. Drag and Drop 79
    3.7. Copy and Paste 79
    3.8. Image Browser 79

Chapter 6: Getting Images out of GIMP 80
1. Files 80
    1.1. Save / Export Images 80
    1.2. File Formats 80
2. Preparing your Images for the Web 91
    2.1. Images with an Optimal Size/Quality Ratio 92
    2.2. Reducing the File Size Even More 93
    2.3. Saving Images with Transparency 93

Chapter 7: Painting with GIMP 96
1. The Selection 96
    1.1. Feathering 98
    1.2. Making a Selection Partially Transparent 99
2. Creating and Using Selections 100
    2.1. Moving a Selection 100
    2.2. Adding or subtracting selections 102
3. The QuickMask 103
    3.1. Overview 103

    3.2. Properties 104
  4. Using QuickMask Mode 104
  5. Paths 105
    5.1. Path Creation 105
    5.2. Path Properties 107
    5.3. Paths and Selections 108
    5.4. Transforming Paths 108
    5.5. Stroking a Path 109
    5.6. Paths and Text 111
    5.7. Paths and SVG files 111
  6. Brushes 112
  7. Adding New Brushes 115
  8. The GIH Dialog Box 116
  9. Varying brush size 125
    9.1. How to vary the height of a brush 125
    9.2. Creating a brush quickly 127
  10. Gradients 128
  11. Patterns 132
  12. Palettes 136
    12.1. Colormap 138
  13. Presets 139
  14. Drawing Simple Objects 140
    14.1. Drawing a Straight Line 140
    14.2. Creating a Basic Shape 145

Chapter 8: Combining Images 147
  1. Introduction to Layers 147
    1.1. Layer Properties 147
  2. Layer Modes 153
  3. Creating New Layers 181
  4. Layer Groups 182

Chapter 9: Text Management 187
  1. Text Management 187
  2. Text Tool Box 191
    2.1. Text Tool Box Context menu 192
  3. Text 192
    3.1. Embellishing Text 192
    3.2. Adding Fonts 193
    3.3. Font Problems 195

Chapter10: Enhancing Photographs 196
  1. Working with Digital Camera Photos 196
    1.1. Introduction 196
    1.2. Improving Composition 196

v

  1.3. Improving Colors 198
  1.4. Adjusting Sharpness 202
  1.5. Removing Unwanted Objects from an Image 203
  1.6. Saving Your Results 205

Chapter 11: Color Management with GIMP 208
 1. Color Management in GIMP 208
  1.1. Problems of a non Color Managed Workflow 209
  1.2. Introduction to a Color Managed Workflow 210

Chapter 12: Enrich my GIMP 212
 1. Preferences Dialog 212
  1.1. Introduction 212
  1.2. Environment 213
  1.3. Interface 215
  1.4. Theme 217
  1.5. Help System 218
  1.6. Tool Options 219
  1.7. Toolbox 221
  1.8. Default Image Preferences 223
  1.9. Default Image Grid 224
  1.10. Image Windows 225
  1.11. Image Window Appearance 227
  1.12. Image Window Title and Status bar 228
  1.13. Display 230
  1.14. Color Management 232
  1.15. Input Devices 235
  1.16. Input Controllers 237
  1.17. Window Management 241
  1.18. Folders 243
  1.19. Data Folders 244
 2. Grids and Guides 245
  2.1. The Image Grid 246
  2.2. Guides 247
 3. Rendering a Grid 248
 4. How to Set Your Tile Cache 248
 5. Creating Shortcuts to Menu Functions 251
 6. Customize Splash-Screen 253

Chapter 13: Scripting 254
 1. Plugins 254
  1.1. Introduction 254
  1.2. Using Plugins 255
  1.3. Installing New Plugins 256
  1.4. Writing Plugins 258

2. Using Script-Fu Scripts 258
2.1. Script-Fu? 258
2.2. Installing Script-Fus 259
2.3. Do's and Don'ts 259
2.4. Different Kinds Of Script-Fus 259
2.5. Standalone Scripts 261
2.6. Image-Dependent Scripts 263
3. A Script-Fu Tutorial 263
3.1. Getting Acquainted With Scheme 263
3.2. Variables And Functions 266
3.3. Lists, Lists And More Lists 269
3.4. Your First Script-Fu Script 273
3.5. Giving Our Script Some Guts 281
3.6. Extending The Text Box Script 285
3.7. Your script and its working 288

Appendix i
The Very Beginning of GIMP i
The Early Days of GIMP ii
How to Receive Your Part III (Three) PDF Copy iv

Part I:

Getting Started

Chapter 1. Introduction

1. Welcome to GIMP

GIMP is a multi-platform photo manipulation tool. GIMP is an acronym for GNU Image Manipulation Program. The GIMP is suitable for a variety of image manipulation tasks, including photo retouching, image composition, and image construction.

GIMP has many capabilities. It can be used as a simple paint program, an expert quality photo retouching program, an online batch processing system, a mass production image renderer, an image format converter, etc.

GIMP is expandable and extensible. It is designed to be augmented with plug-ins and extensions to do just about anything. The advanced scripting interface allows everything from the simplest task to the most complex image manipulation procedures to be easily scripted.

One of The GIMP's strengths is its free availability from many sources for many operating systems. Most GNU/Linux distributions include The GIMP as a standard application. The GIMP is also available for other operating systems such as Microsoft Windows™ or Apple's Mac OS X™ (Darwin). The GIMP is a Free Software application covered by the General Public License [GPL]. The GPL provides users with the freedom to access and alter the source code that makes up computer programs.

1.1. Authors

The first version of the GIMP was written by Peter Mattis and Spencer Kimball. Many other developers have contributed more recently, and thousands have provided support and testing. GIMP releases are currently being orchestrated by Sven Neumann and Mitch Natterer and the other members of the GIMP-Team.

1.2. The GIMP Help system

The GIMP Documentation Team and other users have provided you with the information necessary to understand how to use GIMP. The User Manual is an important part of this help. The current version is on the web site of the Documentation Team [GIMP-DOCS] in HTML format. The HTML version is also available as context sensitive help (if you installed it) while using GIMP by pressing the **F1** key. Help on specific menu items can be accessed by pressing the **F1** key while the mouse pointer is focused on the menu item. Read on to begin your GIMP journey.

1.3. Features and Capabilities

The following list is a short overview of some of the features and capabilities which GIMP offers you:

- A full suite of painting tools including brushes, a pencil, an airbrush, cloning, etc.
- Tile-based memory management, so image size is limited only by available disk space
- Sub-pixel sampling for all paint tools for high-quality anti-aliasing
- Full Alpha channel support for working with transparency
- Layers and channels
- A procedural database for calling internal GIMP functions from external programs, such as Script-Fu
- Advanced scripting capabilities
- Multiple undo/redo (limited only by disk space)
- Transformation tools including rotate, scale, shear and flip
- Support for a wide range of file formats, including GIF, JPEG, PNG, XPM, TIFF, TGA, MPEG, PS, PDF, PCX, BMP and many others
- Selection tools, including rectangle, ellipse, free, fuzzy, bezier and intelligent scissors
- Plug-ins that allow for the easy addition of new file formats and new effect filters.

2. What's New in GIMP 2.8?

GIMP 2.8 is another important release from a development point of view, even more that it was for 2.6. It features a big change to the user interface addressing one of the most often received complaints: the lack of a single window mode. Moreover the integration effort of GEGL library had taken a big step forward, reaching more than 90% of the GIMP core, a new powerful transformation tool, layer groups, new common options, new brushes, improved text tool, and more.

User Interface

New single window mode

With this new feature it will be possible to work with all the GIMP dialogs inside one big window, usually with the image(s) centered inside. No more floating panels or toolbox but the dialogs could be arranged inside this single window. This mode could be enabled or disabled all the time, even while working, and the option will be remembered through the sessions.

Figure 1.1. The new look of the single window mode

New file save workflow

> Now Save and Save as work only with xcf formats. If you want to export an image in another format, say jpg or png, you have to explicitly Export it. This enhances the workflow and lets you simply overwrite the original file or export to various other formats.

Figure 1.2. The new image workflow

New image bar

A new useful image bar comes with the single window mode, which lets you switch easily between open images through the means of a tab bar with image thumbnails.

Figure 1.3. The new image bar

New arrangement options

>GIMP will make users working with two screens (one for dialogs, the other for images) happy: now it is possible to arrange the dialogs one over the other, in tabs and in columns too.

Figure 1.4. Multi column docks

New resources tags

>GIMP Brushes, Gradients, Pattern and Palettes can be filtered and searched via tags. Tags are text labels that the user can assign to resources. With Tags the user can easily find the resources by means of an input text box. Tags can be manually assigned by the user with the same input box used for searching tags, or they can be automatically tagged using the directory name of the imported items.

Figure 1.5. Resource tags

Simple math in size entries

Enhancements have also been made to the size entry widget, which is used for inputting most of the x, y, width, height parameters. For example, in the scale dialog it is now possible to write "50%" in the Width field to scale the image to 50% of the width. Expressions such as "30in + 40px" and "4 * 5.4in" work, too.

Figure 1.6. Math size entries

Minor changes

- The new "Lock Pixels" option in the layers dialog can avoid undesired painting on a layer when working with several layers.

Figure 1.7. The new Lock Pixels option

- Now you can move between images in single and multi window mode using the shortcuts **Ctrl+PageUp/PageDown** or **Alt+Number**.
- Add support for F2 to rename items in lists.
- You can now **Alt+Click** on layers in the Layers dialog to create a selection from it. Add, subtract and intersect modifiers **Click**, **Shift** and **Ctrl+Shift** keys work too. This makes it easy to compose contents of a layer based on the contents of other layers, without detours.
- Since the keyboard shortcuts **Ctrl+E** and **Ctrl+Shift+E** have been redirected to image export mechanisms, new keyboard shortcuts have been setup for "Shrink Wrap" and "Fit in Window", namely **Ctrl+J** and **Ctrl+Shift+J** respectively.
- Added Windows → Hide docks menu item that does what "Tab" does and also displays its state, which is now persistent across sessions, too.
- The layer modes have been rearranged into more logical and useful groups based on the effect they have on layers. Layer modes that make the layer lighter are in one group, layer modes that make the layer darker in another group, and so forth.
- In multi-window mode, you can now close the Toolbox without quitting GIMP.
- Allow binding arbitrary actions to extra mouse buttons.
- Now it is possible to change the application language directly from the preference menu.

Tools, Filters and Plug-ins

A new tool: Cage Transform

With this new tool is now possible to create custom bending of a selection just moving control points. This is the result of one of our Google Summer of Code 2010 students.

Figure 1.8. Cage Transform

Improved Text Tool

The text tool has been enhanced to support on canvas text writing and make possible changing the attributes of a single char.

Figure 1.9. Improved text tool

New layer groups

It is now possible to group set of layers and treat them like an entity. It is possible to switch a group on or off and to move the group in the layers dialog. It is easy to add / remove existing layers to a group or to create / delete a layer inside the group and it is even possible to create embedded groups of groups. It is possible to apply a layer mode to a group as you do with a single layer. All this greatly improves the workflow with complex multilayer images making them easier to manage.

Figure 1.10. New layer groups

Rotating brushes

Brushes can now be rotated at will, acting on the brush option "Angle".

Figure 1.11. Rotating brushes

Minor changes

- The default Quick Mask color is now configurable.
- The RTL mode (right to left writing) has been improved in the Text tool.
- You can specify the written language in the Text Tool. This helps choosing an appropriate font, or appropriate glyphs for the selected language.
- Added optional diagonal guides to the crop tool.
- Added "Rule of fifths" crop guide overlay.
- A Cairo based PDF exporter has been implemented. Although being somewhat simplistic, the exporter saves text, embedding fonts into the final PDF file, and attempts to convert bitmaps to vector objects.
- Brush dynamics improved.
- Added plug-in for loading JPEG2000 images.
- Added plug-ins for X11 Mouse Cursor import and export support.
- Added fundamental OpenRaster (.ora) import and export support.
- Added RGB565 support to the csource plug-in.
- Added a new "Create" command that allows loading a Web page directly into GIMP using Webkit.

Under the Hood

GEGL

The porting of the GIMP core towards the new high bit-depth and non-destructive editing GEGL. GEGL library has taken big steps and now more than 90% of the task is already finished.

In addition to porting color operations to GEGL, an experimental GEGL Operation tool has been added, found in the Tools menu. It enables applying GEGL operations to an image and it gives on-canvas previews of the results. The screenshot below shows this for a Gaussian Blur.

Figure 1.12. GEGL operation

Cairo porting

> Started with GIMP version 2.6, all tools rendering on canvas is now completely ported to CAIRO. It provides smooth antialiased graphics and improves GIMP look. Some plug-ins have been upgraded to Cairo as well. Additionally all tools now use an on-canvas progress indicator instead of the one in the statusbar.

Figure 1.13. Progress indicator

Miscellaneous

License change

> The GIMP license has been changed to (L)GPLv3+.

New script API

- A lot of GIMP APIs have been rebuilt to simplify developing new scripts.
- To further enhances scripting abilities, API changes to support layer groups have been made.

Backwards Compatibility

To allow migrating from the old tools presets system to the new one, there is a Python script, which you can download from the GIMP wiki site. However, the old tools presets are not 100% convertible to the new tool presets. For instance, brush scale from 2.6 can't be converted to brush size in 2.8.

Known Problems

Working with graphics tablets could be problematic due to the GTK+2 library in use. If in this case either use the older version 2.6 or wait for the up coming version 3.0 for the full GTK+3 support.

Chapter 2. Fire up the GIMP

1. Running GIMP

Most often, you start GIMP either by clicking on an icon (if your system is set up to provide you with one), or by typing **gimp** on a command line. If you have multiple versions of GIMP installed, you may need to type **gimp-2.8** to get the latest version. You can, if you want, give a list of image files on the command line after the program name, and they will automatically be opened by GIMP as it starts. It is also possible, though, to open files from within GIMP once it is running.

Most operating systems support file associations, which associates a class of files (as determined by their filename extension, such as .jpg) with a corresponding application (such as GIMP). When image files are properly "associated" to GIMP, you can double click on an image to open it in GIMP.

1.1. Known Platforms

The GIMP is the most widely supported image manipulation available today. The platforms on which GIMP is known to work include:

GNU/Linux™, Apple Mac OS X™, Microsoft Windows™, OpenBSD™, NetBSD™, FreeBSD™, Solaris™, SunOS™, AIX™, HP-UX™, Tru64™, Digital UNIX™, OSF/1™, IRIX™, OS/2™, and BeOS™.

The GIMP is easily ported to other operating systems because of its source code availability. For further information visit the GIMP developers homepage. GIMP-DEV.

1.2. Language

GIMP automatically detects and uses the system language. In the unlikely event that language detection fails, or if you just want to use a different language, since GIMP-2.8, you can do so through: Edit → Preferences → Interface.

You can also use:

Under Linux

> *In LINUX*: in console mode, type **LANGUAGE=en gimp** or **LANG=en gimp** replacing en by fr, de, ... according to the language you want.

Background: Using **LANGUAGE=en** sets an environment variable for the executed program **gimp**.

Under Windows XP

Control Panel → System → Advanced → Environment button in "System Variables" area: Add button: Enter LANG for Name and fr or de... for Value. Watch out! You have to click on three successive OK to validate your choice.

If you change languages often, you can create a batch file to change the language. Open NotePad. Type the following commands (for french for instance):

set lang=fr
start gimp-2.8.exe

Save this file as GIMP-FR.BAT (or another name, but always with a .BAT extension). Create a shortcut and drag it to your desktop.

Another possibility: Start → Programs → GTK Runtime Environment Then Select language and select the language you want in the drop-down list.

Under Apple Mac OS X

From System Preferences, click on the International icon. In the Language tab, the desired language should be the first in the list.

Another GIMP instance

Use **-n** to run multiple instances of GIMP. For example, use **gimp-2.8** to start GIMP in the default system language, and **LANGUAGE=en gimp-2.8 -n** to start another instance of GIMP in English; this is very useful for translators.

1.3. Command Line Arguments

Although arguments are not required when starting GIMP, the most common arguments are shown below. On a Unix system, you can use **man gimp** for a complete list.

Command line arguments must be in the command line that you use to start GIMP as **gimp-2.8 [OPTION...] [FILE|URI...]**.

-?, --help

> Display a list of all commandline options.

--help-all

> Show all help options.

--help-gtk

> Show GTK+ Options.

-v, --version

> Print the GIMP version and exit.

--license

> Show license information and exit.

--verbose

> Show detailed start-up messages.

-n, --new-instance

> Start a new GIMP instance.

-a, --as-new

> Open images as new.

-i, --no-interface

> Run without a user interface.

-d, --no-data

> Do not load patterns, gradients, palettes, or brushes. Often useful in non-interactive situations where start-up time is to be minimized.

-f, --no-fonts

> Do not load any fonts. This is useful to load GIMP faster for scripts that do not use fonts, or to find problems related to malformed fonts that hang GIMP.

-s, --no-splash

Do not show the splash screen while starting.

--no-shm

Do not use shared memory between GIMP and plugins.

--no-cpu-accel

Do not use special CPU acceleration functions. Useful for finding or disabling buggy accelerated hardware or functions.

--session=*name*

Use a different sessionrc for this GIMP session. The given session name is appended to the default sessionrc filename.

--gimprc=filename

Use an alternative gimprc instead of the default one. The gimprc file contains a record of your preferences. Useful in cases where plugins paths or machine specs may be different.

--system-gimprc=*filename*

Use an alternate system gimprc file.

-b, --batch=*commands*

Execute the set of commands non-interactively. The set of commands is typically in the form of a script that can be executed by one of the GIMP scripting extensions. When the command is -, commands are read from standard input.

--batch-interpreter=*proc*

Specify the procedure to use to process batch commands. The default procedure is Script-Fu.

--console-messages

Do not popup dialog boxes on errors or warnings. Print the messages on the console instead.

--pdb-compat-mode=*mode*

PDB compatibility mode (off|on|warn).

--stack-trace-mode=*mode*

Debug in case of a crash (never|query|always).

--debug-handlers

Enable non-fatal debugging signal handlers. Useful for GIMP debugging.

--g-fatal-warnings

Make all warnings fatal. Useful for debug.

--dump-gimprc

Output a gimprc file with default settings. Useful if you messed up the gimprc file.

--display=*display*

Use the designated X display (does not apply to all platforms).

2. Starting GIMP the first time

When first run, GIMP performs a series of steps to configure options and directories. The configuration process creates a subdirectory in your home directory called .gimp-2.8. All of the configuration information is stored in this directory. If you remove or rename the directory, GIMP will repeat the initial configuration process, creating a new .gimp-2.8 directory. Use this capability to explore different configuration options without destroying your existing installation, or to recover if your configuration files are damaged.

2.1. Finally . . .

Just a couple of suggestions before you start, though: First, GIMP provides tips you can read at any time using the menu command Help → Tip of the Day. The tips provide information that is considered useful, but not easy to learn by experimenting; so they are worth reading. Please read the tips when you have the time. Second, if at some point you are trying to do something, and GIMP seems to have suddenly stopped functioning, the section Getting Unstuck may help you out. Happy Gimping!

Chapter 3. First Steps with Wilber

1. Basic Concepts

Figure 3.1. Wilber, the GIMP mascot

The Wilber_Construction_Kit (in src/images/) allows you to give the mascot a different appearance. It is the work of Tuomas Kuosmanen (tigertATgimp.org).

This section provides a brief introduction to the basic concepts and terminology used in GIMP. The concepts presented here are explained in much greater depth elsewhere. With a few exceptions, we have avoided cluttering this section with a lot of links and cross-references: everything mentioned here is so high-level that you can easily locate it in the index.

Images

> Images are the basic entities used by GIMP. Roughly speaking, an "image" corresponds to a single file, such as a TIFF or JPEG file. You can also think of an image as corresponding to a single display window (although in truth it is possible to have multiple windows all displaying the same image). It is not possible to have a single window display more than one image, though, or for an image to have no window displaying it.
>
> A GIMP image may be quite a complicated thing. Instead of thinking of it as a sheet of paper with a picture on it, think of it as more like a stack of sheets, called "layers". In addition to a stack of layers, a GIMP image may contain a selection mask, a set of channels, and a set of

paths. In fact, GIMP provides a mechanism for attaching arbitrary pieces of data, called "parasites", to an image.

In GIMP, it is possible to have many images open at the same time. Although large images may use many megabytes of memory, GIMP uses a sophisticated tile-based memory management system that allows GIMP to handle very large images gracefully. There are limits, however, and having more memory available may improve system performance.

Layers

If a simple image can be compared to a single sheet of paper, an image with layers is likened to a sheaf of transparent papers stacked one on top of the other. You can draw on each paper, but still see the content of the other sheets through the transparent areas. You can also move one sheet in relation to the others. Sophisticated GIMP users often deal with images containing many layers, even dozens of them. Layers need not be opaque, and they need not cover the entire extent of an image, so when you look at an image's display, you may see more than just the top layer: you may see elements of many layers.

Resolution

Digital images comprise of a grid of square elements of varying colors, called pixels. Each image has a pixel size, such as 900 pixels wide by 600 pixels high. But pixels don't have a set size in physical space. To set up an image for printing, we use a value called resolution, defined as the ratio between an image's size in pixels and its physical size (usually in inches) when it is printed on paper. Most file formats (but not all) can save this value, which is expressed as ppi — pixels per inch. When printing a file, the resolution value determines the size the image will have on paper, and as a result, the physical size of the pixels. The same 900x600 pixel image may be printed as a small 3x2" card with barely noticeable pixels — or as a large poster with large, chunky pixels. Images imported from cameras and mobile devices tend to have a resolution value attached to the file. The value is usually 72 or 96ppi. It is important to realize that this value is arbitrary and was chosen for historic reasons. You can always change the resolution value inside GIMP — this has no effect on the actual image pixels. Furthermore, for uses such as displaying images on line, on mobile devices, television or video games — in short, any use that is not print — the resolution value is meaningless and is ignored, and instead the image is usually displayed so that each image pixel conforms to one screen pixel.

Channels

A Channel is a single component of a pixel's color. For a colored pixel in GIMP, these components are usually Red, Green, Blue and sometimes transparency (Alpha). For a Grayscale image, they are Gray and Alpha and for an Indexed color image, they are Indexed and Alpha.

The entire rectangular array of any one of the color components for all of the pixels in an image is also referred to as a Channel. You can see these color channels with the Channels dialog.

When the image is displayed, GIMP puts these components together to form the pixel colors for the screen, printer, or other output device. Some output devices may use different channels from Red, Green and Blue. If they do, GIMP's channels are converted into the appropriate ones for the device when the image is displayed.

Channels can be useful when you are working on an image which needs adjustment in one particular color. For example, if you want to remove "red eye" from a photograph, you might work on the Red channel.

You can look at channels as masks which allow or restrict the output of the color that the channel represents. By using Filters on the channel information, you can create many varied and subtle effects on an image. A simple example of using a Filter on the color channels is the Channel Mixer filter.

In addition to these channels, GIMP also allows you to create other channels (or more correctly, Channel Masks), which are displayed in the lower part of the Channels dialog. You can create a New Channel or save a selection to a channel (mask). See the glossary entry on Masks for more information about Channel Masks.

Selections

Often when modify an image, you only want a part of the image to be affected. The "selection" mechanism makes this possible. Each image has its own selection, which you normally see as a moving dashed line separating the selected parts from the unselected parts (the so-called "marching ants"). Actually this is a bit misleading: selection in GIMP is graded, not all-or-nothing, and really the selection is represented by a full-fledged grayscale channel. The dashed line that you normally see is simply a contour line at the 50%-selected level. At any time, though, you can visualize the selection channel in all its glorious detail by toggling the **QuickMask** button.

A large component of learning how to use GIMP effectively is acquiring the art of making good selections—selections that contain exactly what you need and nothing more. Because selection-handling is so centrally important, GIMP provides many tools for doing it: an assortment of selection-making tools, a menu of selection operations, and the ability to switch to Quick Mask mode, in which you can treat the selection channel as though it were a color channel, thereby "painting the selection".

Undoing

When you make mistakes, you can undo them. Nearly everything you can do to an image is undoable. In fact, you can usually undo a substantial number of the most recent things you did, if you decide that they were misguided. GIMP makes this possible by keeping a history of your actions. This history consumes memory, though, so undoability is not infinite. Some actions use very little undo memory, so that you can do dozens of them before the earliest ones are deleted from this history; other types of actions require massive amounts of undo memory. You can configure the amount of memory GIMP allows for the undo history of each image, but in any situation, you should always be able to undo at least your 2-3 most recent actions. (The most important action that is not undoable is closing an image. For this reason, GIMP asks you to confirm that you really want to close the image if you have made any changes to it.)

Plug-ins

Many, probably most, of the things that you do to an image in GIMP are done by the GIMP application itself. However, GIMP also makes extensive use of "plug-ins", which are external programs that interact very closely with GIMP, and are capable of manipulating images and other GIMP objects in very sophisticated ways. Many important plug-ins are bundled with GIMP, but there are also many available by other means. In fact, writing plug-ins (and scripts) is the easiest way for people not on the GIMP development team to add new capabilities to GIMP.

All of the commands in the Filters menu, and a substantial number of commands in other menus, are actually implemented as plug-ins.

Scripts

In addition to plug-ins, which are programs written in the C language, GIMP can also make use of scripts. The largest number of existing scripts are written in a language called Script-Fu, which is unique to

GIMP (for those who care, it is a dialect of the Lisp-like language called Scheme). It is also possible to write GIMP scripts in Python or Perl. These languages are more flexible and powerful than Script-Fu; their disadvantage is that they depend on software that does not automatically come packaged with GIMP, so they are not guaranteed to work correctly in every GIMP installation.

2. Main Windows

The GIMP user interface is now available in two modes:

- multi-window mode,
- single window mode.

When you open GIMP for the first time, it opens in multi-window mode by default. You can enable single-window mode through Windows → >Single-Window Mode) in the image menu bar. After quitting GIMP with this option enabled, GIMP will start in single-window mode next time.

Multi-Window Mode

Figure 3.2. A screenshot illustrating the multi-window mode.

The screenshot above shows the most basic arrangement of GIMP windows that can be used effectively.

You can notice two panels, left and right, and an image window in middle. A second image is partially masked. The left panel collects

Toolbox and Tool Options dialog together. The right panel collects layers, channels, paths, undo history dialogs together in a multi-tab dock, brushes, patterns and gradients dialogs together in another dock below. You can move these panels on screen. You can also mask them using the **Tab** key.

1. *The Main Toolbox:* Contains a set of icon buttons used to select tools. By default, it also contains the foreground and background colors. You can add brush, pattern, gradient and active image icons. Use Edit → Preferences → Toolbox to enable, or disable the extra items.
2. *Tool options:* Docked below the main Toolbox is a Tool Options dialog, showing options for the currently selected tool (in this case, the Move tool).
3. *Image windows:* Each image open in GIMP is displayed in a separate window. Many images can be open at the same time, limited by only the system resources. Before you can do anything useful in GIMP, you need to have at least one image window open. The image window holds the Menu of the main commands of GIMP (File, Edit, Select...), which you can also get by right-clicking on the window.

    An image can be bigger than the image window. In that case, GIMP displays the image in a reduced zoom level which allows to see the full image in the image window. If you turn to the 100% zoom level, scroll bars appear, allowing you to pan across the image.

4. The *Layers, Channels, Paths, Undo History* dock — note that the dialogs in the dock are tabs. The Layers tab is open : it shows the layer structure of the currently active image, and allows it to be manipulated in a variety of ways. It is possible to do a few very basic things without using the Layers dialog, but even moderately sophisticated GIMP users find it indispensable to have the Layers dialog available at all times.
5. *Brushes/Patterns/Gradients:* The docked dialog below the layer dialog shows the dialogs (tabs) for managing brushes, patterns and gradients.

Dialog and dock managing is described in Section 2.3, "Dialogs and Docking".

Single Window Mode

Figure 3.3. A screenshot illustrating the single-window mode.

You find the same elements, with differences in their management:

- Left and right panels are fixed; you can't move them. But you can decrease or increase their width. If you reduce the width of a multi-tab dock, there may be not enough place for all tabs; then arrow-heads appear allowing you to scroll through tabs.

  As in multi-window mode, you can mask these panels using the **Tab** key.

- The image window occupies all space between both panels.

  When several images are open, a new bar appears above the image window, with a tab for every image. You can navigate between images by clicking on tabs or either using **Ctrl+PageUp or PageDown** or **Alt+Number**. "Number" is tab number; you must use the number keys of the upper line of your keyboard, not that of keypad (Alt-shift necessary for some national keyboards).

This is a minimal setup. There are over a dozen other types of dialogs used by GIMP for various purposes, but users typically open them when they need them and close them when they are done. Knowledgeable users generally keep the Toolbox (with Tool Options) and Layers dialog open at all times. The Toolbox is essential to many GIMP operations. The Tool Options section is actually a separate dialog, shown docked to the Main Toolbox in the screenshot. Knowledgeable users almost always have it set up this way: it is very difficult to use tools effectively without being able to see how their options are set. The Layers dialog comes into play when you work with an image with multiple layers: after you advance beyond the most basic stages of GIMP expertise, this means *almost always*. And of course it helps to display the images you're editing on the screen; if you close the image window before saving your work, GIMP will ask you whether you want to close the file.

Note

If your GIMP layout is lost, your arrangement is easy to recover using Windows → Recently Closed Docks ; the Windows menu command is only available while an image is open. To add, close, or detach a tab from a dock, click ◁ in the upper right corner of a dialog. This opens the Tab menu. Select Add Tab, Close Tab , or Detach Tab.

The following sections walk you through the components of each of the windows shown in the screenshot, explaining what they are and how they work. Once you have read them, plus the section describing the basic structure of GIMP images, you should have learned enough to use GIMP for a wide variety of basic image manipulations. You can then look through the rest of the manual at your leisure (or just experiment) to learn the almost limitless number of more subtle and specialized things that are possible. Have fun!

2.1. The Toolbox

Figure 3.4. Screenshot of the Toolbox

The Toolbox is the heart of GIMP. Here is a quick tour of what you will find there.

> **Tip**
>
> In the Toolbox, as in most parts of GIMP, moving the mouse over something and letting it rest for a moment, usually displays a "tooltip" that describes the thing. Short cut keys are also frequently shown in the tooltip. In many cases, you can hover the mouse over an item and press the **F1** key to get help about the thing that is underneath the mouse.

By default, only the Foreground-background icon is visible. You can add Brush-Pattern-Gradient icons and Active Image icon through Edit → Preferences → Toolbox: Tools configuration.

1. *Tool icons:* These icons are buttons which activate tools for a wide variety of purposes: selecting parts of images, painting an image, transforming an image, etc. Section 1, "**The Toolbox**" gives an overview of how to work with tools, and each tool is described systematically in the Tools chapter.
2. *Foreground/Background colors:* The color areas here show you GIMP's current foreground and background colors, which come into play in many operations. Clicking on either one of them brings up a color selector dialog that allows you to change to a different color. Clicking on the double-headed arrow swaps the two colors, and clicking on the small symbol in the lower left corner resets them to black and white.
3. *Brush/Pattern/Gradient:* The symbols here show you GIMP's current selections for: the Paintbrush, used by all tools that allow you to paint on the image ("painting" includes operations like erasing and smudging, by the way); for the Pattern, which is used in filling selected areas of an image; and for the Gradient, which comes into play whenever an operation requires a smoothly varying range of colors. Clicking on any of these symbols brings up a dialog window that allows you to change it.
4. *Active Image:* In GIMP, you can work with many images at once, but at any given moment, only one image is the "active image". Here you find a small iconic representation of the active image. Click the icon to display a dialog with a list of the currently open images, click an image in the dialog to make it active. Usually, you click an image window in multi-window mode, or an image tab in single-window mode, to make it the active image.

   You can "Drop to an XDS file manager to save the image". XDS is an acronym for "X Direct Save Protocol": an additional feature for the X

Window System graphical user interface for Unix-like operating systems.

Note

At every start, GIMP selects a tool (the brush), a color, a brush and a pattern by default, always the same. If you want GIMP to select the last tool, color, brush and pattern you used when quitting your previous session, check the Save input device settings on exit in Preferences/Input Devices.

Tip

The Toolbox window displays "Wilber's eyes" along the top of the dialog. You can get rid of the "Wilber's eyes" by adding the following line to your gimprc file: (toolbox-wilber no). It only affects the toolbox. The eyes in the Image window are only visible when you do not have an open image.

Tip

Drag and drop an image from a file browser into the Toolbox window to open the image in its own Image window or tab.

2.2. Image Window

GIMP user interface is now available in two modes: multi-window mode (default), and single-window mode (optional, through Windows → >Single-Window Mode. But, if you quit GIMP with this option enabled, GIMP will open in single mode next time).

In single-window mode, no new window is added: images and dialogs are added in tabs. Please see **Single Window Mode.**

When you start GIMP without any image open, the image window seems to be absent in single-window mode, while, in multi-window mode, an image window exists, even if no image is open.

We will begin with a brief description of the components that are present by default in an ordinary image window. Some of the components can be removed by using commands in the View menu.

Figure 3.5. The Image Window in Multi-Window Mode

Figure 3.6. The Image Area in Single-Window Mode

> **Note**
>
> Despite *Single*-window Mode, we will use "image window" for "image area".

1. *Title Bar:* The Title Bar in an image window without an image displays "GNU Image Manipulating Program". An image window with an image displays the image name and its specifications in the title bar according to the settings in Preference Dialog. The Title Bar is provided by the operating system, not by GIMP, so its appearance is likely to vary with the operating system, window manager, and/or

theme — in Linux systems, this title bar has a button to display the image window on all your desktops. You also have this button in toolbox window and layer window.

If you have opened a non-xcf image, it is "(imported)" as a .xcf file and its original name appears in the status bar at the bottom of the image window.

When an image is modified, an asterisk appears in front of title.

2. *Image Menu:* Directly below the Title Bar appears the Menu bar (unless it has been suppressed). The Image Menu provides access to nearly every operation you can perform on an image. You can also right-click on an image to display a pop-up image menu, [1], or by left-clicking on the little "arrow-head" symbol in the upper left corner, called *Menu Button*, described just below. Many menu commands are also associated with keyboard *shortcuts* as shown in the menu. You can define your own custom shortcuts for menu actions, if you enable Use Dynamic Keyboard Shortcuts in the Preferences dialog.
3. *Menu Button:* Click the Menu Button to display the Image Menu in a column,(essential in full screen mode). If you like to use keyboard shortcuts, use **Shift+F10** to open the menu.
4. *Ruler:* In the default layout, rulers are shown above and to the left of the image. Use the rulers to determine coordinates within the image. The default unit for rulers is pixels; use the settings described below to use a unit other than pixels.

    One of the most important uses of rulers is to create *guides*. Click and drag a ruler into the image to create a guide. A guide is a line that helps you accurately position things—or verify that another line is truly horizontal or vertical. Click and drag a guide to move it. Drag a guide out of the image to delete it; you can always drag another guide into the image. You can even use multiple guides at the same time.

    In ruler area, the mouse pointer position is marked with two small arrow-heads pointing vertically and horizontally.

5. *QuickMask Toggle:* The small button in the lower left corner of the image toggles the Quick Mask on and off. When the Quick Mask is on, the button is outlined in red. See **QuickMask** for more details on this highly useful tool.
6. *Pointer Coordinates:* When the pointer (mouse cursor, if you are using a mouse) is within the image boundaries, the rectangular area in the lower left corner of the window displays the current pointer coordinates. The units are the same as for the rulers.

7. *Units Menu:* Use the Units Menu to change the units used for rulers and several other purposes. The default unit is pixels, but you can quickly change to inches, cm, or several other possibilities using this menu. Note that the setting of "Dot for dot" in the View menu affects how the display is scaled: see **Dot for Dot** for more information.
8. *Zoom Button:* There are a number of ways to zoom the image in or out, but the Zoom Button is perhaps the simplest. You can directly enter a zoom level in the text box for precise control.
9. *Status Area:* The Status Area is at the bottom of the image window. By default, the Status Area displays the original name of the image.xcf file, and the amount of system memory used by the image. Please use Edit → Preferences → Image Windows → Title & Status to customize the information displayed in the Status Area. During time-consuming operations, the status area temporarily shows the running operation and how complete the operation is.

   Note

   Note that the memory used by the image is very different from the image file size. For instance, a 70Kb .PNG image may occupy 246Kb in RAM when displayed. There are two primary reasons the difference in memory usage. First, a .PNG file is compressed format, and the image is reconstituted in RAM in uncompressed form. Second, GIMP uses extra memory, and copies of the image, for use by the Undo command.

10. *Cancel Button:* During complex time-consuming operations, usually a plug-in, a Cancel button temporarily appears in the lower right corner of the window. Use the Cancel button to stop the operation.

    Note

    A few plug-ins respond badly to being canceled, sometimes leaving corrupted pieces of images behind.

11. *Navigation Control:* This is a small cross-shaped button at the lower right corner of the image display. Click and hold (do not release the mouse button) on the navigation control to display the Navigation Preview. The Navigation Preview has a miniature view of the image with the displayed area outlined. Use the Navigation Preview to quickly pan to a different part of the image—move the mouse while keeping the button pressed. The Navigation Window is often the most convenient way to quickly navigate around a large image with only a small portion displayed. (See **Navigation Dialog** for other ways to

access the Navigation Window). (If your mouse has a middle-button, click-drag with it to pan across the image).
12. *Inactive Padding Area:* When the image dimensions are smaller than the image window, this padding area separates the active image display and the inactive padding area, so you're able to distinguish between them. You cannot apply any Filters or Operations in general to the inactive area.
13. *Image Display:* The most important part of the image window is, of course, the image display or canvas. It occupies the central area of the window, surrounded by a yellow dotted line showing the image boundary, against a neutral gray background. You can change the zoom level of the image display in a variety of ways, including the Zoom setting described below.
14. *Image Window Resize Toggle:* Without enabling this feature, if you change the size of the image window by click-and-dragging border limits, the image size and zoom does not change. If you make the window larger, for example, then you will see more of the image. If this button is pressed, however, the image resizes when the window resizes so that (mostly) the same portion of the image is displayed before and after the window is resized.

Tip

Drag and drop an image into the Toolbox window from a file browser to open the image in its own Image window or tab.

Dragging an image file into the Layer dialog adds it to the image as a new layer.

Image size and image window size can be different. You can make image fit window, and vice versa, using two keyboard shortcuts:

- **Ctrl+J**: this command keeps the zoom level; it adapts window size to image size. The Shrink Wrap command does the same.
- **Ctrl+Shift+J**: this command modifies the zoom level to adapt the image display to the window.

Users with an Apple Macintosh and a one button mouse can use **Ctrl**+mousebutton instead.

2.3. Dialogs and Docking
2.3.1. Organizing Dialogs

GIMP has great flexibility for arranging dialog on your screen. A "dialog" is a moving window which contains options for a tool or is dedicated to a special task. A "dock" is a container which can hold a collection of persistent dialogs, such as the Tool Options dialog, Brushes dialog, Palette dialog, etc. Docks cannot, however, hold non-persistent dialogs such as the Preferences dialog or an Image window.

GIMP has three default docks:

- the Tool Options dock under the Toolbox in the left panel,
- the Layers, Channels, Paths and Undo dock in the upper part of the right panel,
- the Brushes, Patterns and Gradients dock in the lower part of the right panel.

In these docks, each dialog is in its own tab.

In multi-window mode, the Toolbox is a *utility window* and not a dock. In single-window mode, it belongs to the single window.

Use Windows → Dockable Dialogs to view a list of dockable dialogs. Select a dockable dialog from the list to view the dialog. If the dialog is available in a dock, then it is made visible. If the dialog is not in a dock, the behavior is different in multi and single window modes:

- In multi-window mode, a new window, containing the dialog, appears on the screen.
- In single-window mode, the dialog is automatically docked to the Layers-Undo dock as a tab.

You can click-and-drag a tab and drop it in the wanted place:

- either in the tab bar of a dock, to integrate it in the dialog group,
- or on a docking bar that appears as a blue line when the mouse pointer goes over a dock border, to anchor the dialog to the dock.

In multi-window mode, you can also click on the dialog title and drag it to the wanted place.

Figure 3.7. Integrating a new dialog in a dialog group

Here, in multi-window mode, the Histogram dialog was dragged to the tab bar of the Layers-Undo dock.

More simple: the **Add tab** command in the Tab menu **Section 2.3.2, "Tab Menu"**.

Figure 3.8. Anchoring a dialog to a dock border

The Histogram dialog dragged to the left vertical docking bar of the right panel and the result: the dialog anchored to the left border of the right panel. This dialog now belongs to the right panel.

So, you can arrange dialogs in a *multi-column* display, interesting if you work with two screens, one for dialogs, the other for images.

> **Tip**
>
> Press **TAB** in an Image window to toggle the visibility of the docks. This is useful if the docks hide a portion of the image Window. You can quickly hide all the docks, do your work, then display all the docs again. Pressing **TAB** inside a dock to navigate through the dock.

2.3.2. Tab Menu

In each dialog, you can access a special menu of tab-related operations by pressing the Tab Menu button, as highlighted in the figure above. Exactly which commands are shown in the menu depends on the active dialog, but they always include operations for creating new tabs, closing or detaching tabs.

The Tab menu gives you access to the following commands:

Context Menu

> At the top of each Tab menu, an entry opens the dialog's context menu, which contains operations specific to that particular type of dialog. For example, the context menu for the Layers tab is Layers Menu, which contains a set of operations for manipulating layers.

Add Tab

> Add Tab opens into a submenu allowing you to add a large variety of dockable dialogs as new tabs.

Close Tab

> Close the dialog. Closing the last dialog in a dock causes the dock itself to close.

Detach Tab

Detach the dialog from the dock, creating a new dock with the detached dialog as its only member. It has the same effect as dragging the tab out of the dock and releasing it at a location where it cannot be docked.

It's a way to create a paradoxical new window in single-window mode!

If the tab is locked, this menu item is insensitive and grayed out.

Lock Tab to Dock

Prevent the dialog from being moved or detached. When activated, Detach Tab is insensitive and grayed out.

Preview Size

Many, but not all, dialogs have Tab menus containing a Preview Size option, which opens into a submenu giving a list of sizes for the items in the dialog (see the figure above). For example, the Brushes dialog shows pictures of all available brushes: the Preview Size determines how large the pictures are. The default is Medium.

Tab Style

Available only when multiple dialogs are in the same dock, Tab Style opens a submenu allowing you to choose the appearance of the tabs at the top (see the figure above). There are five choices, not all are available for every dialog:

Icon

Use an icon to represent the dialog type.

Current Status

Is only available for dialogs that allows you to select something, such as a brush, pattern, gradient, etc. Current Status shows a representation of the currently selected item in the tab top.

Text

Use text to display the dialog type.

Icon and Text

Using both an icon and text results in wider tabs.

Status and Text

> Show the currently selected item and text with the dialog type.

View as List; View as Grid

> These entries are shown in dialogs that allow you to select an item from a set: brushes, patterns, fonts, etc. You can choose to view the items as a vertical list, with the name of each beside it, or as a grid, with representations of the items but no names. Each has its advantages: viewing as a list gives you more information, but viewing as a grid allows you to see more possibilities at once. The default for this varies across dialogs: for brushes and patterns, the default is a grid; for most other things, the default is a list.
>
> When the tree-view is View as List, you can use tags. Please see **Section 3.6, "Tagging".**
>
> You can also use a list search field:
>
> Use **Ctrl+F** to open the list search field. An item must be selected for this command to be effective.
>
> The list search field automatically closes after five seconds if you do nothing.
>
> > **Note**
> >
> > The search field shortcut is also available for the tree-view you get in the "Brush", "Font" or "Pattern" option of several tools.

Show Button Bar

> Some dialogs display a button bar on the bottom of the dialog; for example, the Patterns, Brushes, Gradients, and Images dialogs. This is a toggle. If it is checked, then the Button Bar is displayed.
>
> This option is available in multi-window mode only. This is a toggle. If it is checked, then an Image Menu is shown at the top of the dock:
>
> It is not available for dialogs docked below the Toolbox. This option is interesting only if you have several open images on your screen.

Auto Follow Active Image

This option is available in multi-window mode only. This option is also interesting only if you have several images open on your screen. Then, the information displayed in a dock is always that of the selected image in the Image Selection drop-down list. If the Auto Follow Active Image is disabled, the image can be selected only in the Image Selection. If enabled, you can also select it by activating the image directly (clicking on its title bar).

3. Undoing

Almost anything you do to an image in GIMP can be undone. You can undo the most recent action by choosing Edit → Undo from the image menu, but this is done so frequently that you really should memorize the keyboard shortcut, **Ctrl+Z**.

Undoing can itself be undone. After having undone an action, you can *redo* it by choosing Edit → Redo from the image menu, or use the keyboard shortcut, **Ctrl+Y**. It is often helpful to judge the effect of an action by repeatedly undoing and redoing it. This is usually very quick, and does not consume any extra resources or alter the undo history, so there is never any harm in it.

> **Caution**
>
> If you undo one or more actions and then operate on the image in any way except by using Undo or Redo, it will no longer be possible to redo those actions: they are lost forever. The solution to this, if it creates a problem for you, is to duplicate the image and then test on the copy. (Do *Not* test the original, because the undo/redo history is not copied when you duplicate an image.)

If you often find yourself undoing and redoing many steps at a time, it may be more convenient to work with the **Undo History dialog**, a dockable dialog that shows you a small sketch of each point in the Undo History, allowing you to go back or forward to that point by clicking.

Undo is performed on an image-specific basis: the "Undo History" is one of the components of an image. GIMP allocates a certain amount of memory to each image for this purpose. You can customize your Preferences to increase or decrease the amount, using the **Environment** page of the Preferences dialog. There are two important variables: the *minimal number of undo levels*, which GIMP will maintain regardless of how much memory they consume, and the *maximum undo memory*, beyond which GIMP will begin to delete the oldest items from the Undo History.

Note

Even though the Undo History is a component of an image, it is not saved when you save the image using GIMP's native XCF format, which preserves every other image property. When the image is reopened, it will have an empty Undo History.

GIMP's implementation of Undo is rather sophisticated. Many operations require very little Undo memory (e.g., changing visibility of a layer), so you can perform long sequences of them before they drop out of the Undo History. Some operations, such as changing layer visibility, are *compressed*, so that doing them several times in a row produces only a single point in the Undo History. However, there are other operations that may consume a lot of undo memory. Most filters are implemented by plug-ins, so the GIMP core has no efficient way of knowing what changed. As such, there is no way to implement Undo except by memorizing the entire contents of the affected layer before and after the operation. You might only be able to perform a few such operations before they drop out of the Undo History.

3.1. Things That Cannot be Undone

Most actions that alter an image can be undone. Actions that do not alter the image generally cannot be undone. Examples include saving the image to a file, duplicating the image, copying part of the image to the clipboard, etc. It also includes most actions that affect the image display without altering the underlying image data. The most important example is zooming. There are, however, exceptions: toggling QuickMask on or off can be undone, even though it does not alter the image data.

There are a few important actions that do alter an image but cannot be undone:

Closing the image

> The Undo History is a component of the image, so when the image is closed and all of its resources are freed, the Undo History is gone. Because of this, unless the image has not been modified since the last time it was saved, GIMP always asks you to confirm that you really want to close the image. (You can disable this in the **Environment** page of the Preferences dialog; if you do, you are assuming responsibility for thinking about what you are doing.)

Reverting the image

> "Reverting" means reloading the image from the file. GIMP actually implements this by closing the image and creating a new image, so the Undo History is lost as a consequence. Because of this, if the image is

unclean, GIMP asks you to confirm that you really want to revert the image.

"Pieces" of actions

> Some tools require you to perform a complex series of manipulations before they take effect, but only allow you to undo the whole thing rather than the individual elements. For example, the Intelligent Scissors require you to create a closed path by clicking at multiple points in the image, and then clicking inside the path to create a selection. You cannot undo the individual clicks: undoing after you are finished takes you all the way back to the starting point. For another example, when you are working with the Text tool, you cannot undo individual letters, font changes, etc.: undoing after you are finished removes the newly created text layer.

Filters, and other actions performed by plugins or scripts, can be undone just like actions implemented by the GIMP core, but this requires them to make correct use of GIMP's Undo functions. If the code is not correct, a plugin can potentially corrupt the Undo History, so that not only the plugin but also previous actions can no longer properly be undone. The plugins and scripts distributed with GIMP are all believed to be set up correctly, but obviously no guarantees can be given for plugins you obtain from other sources. Also, even if the code is correct, canceling a plugin while it is running may corrupt the Undo History, so it is best to avoid this unless you have accidentally done something whose consequences are going to be very harmful.

4. Common Tasks

This tutorial is based on text Copyright © 2004 Carol Spears. The original tutorial can be found online: **TUT02**.

4.1. Intention

GIMP is a powerful image editing program with many options and tools. However, it is also well suited for smaller tasks. The following tutorials are meant for those who want to achieve these common tasks without having to learn all the intricacies of GIMP and computer graphics in general.

Hopefully, these tutorials will not only help you with your current task, but also get you ready to learn more complex tools and methods later, when you have the time and inspiration.

All you need to know to start this tutorial, is how to find and open your image. (File → Open from the Image window).

4.2. Change the Size of an Image for the screen

You have a huge image, possibly from a digital camera, and you want to resize it so that it displays nicely on a web page, online board or email message.

Figure 3.17. Example Image for Scaling

The first thing that you might notice after opening the image, is that GIMP opens the image at a logical size for viewing. If your image is very large, like the sample image, GIMP sets the zoom so that it displays nicely on the screen. The zoom level is shown in the status area at the bottom of the Image window. This does not change the actual image.

The other thing to look at in the title-bar is the mode. If the mode shows as RGB in the title bar, you are fine. If the mode says Indexed or Grayscale, read the **Section 4.7, "Change the Mode"**.

Figure 3.18. GIMP Used for Image Scaling

Use Image → Scale Image to open the "Scale Image" dialog. You can right click on the image to open the menu, or use the menu along the top of the Image window. Notice that the "Scale Image" menu item contains three dots, which is a hint that a dialog will be opened.

Figure 3.19. Dialog for Image Scaling in Pixels

The unit of size for the purpose of displaying an image on a screen is the pixel. You can see the dialog has two sections: one for width and height and another for resolution. Resolution applies to printing only and has no effect on the image's size when it is displayed on a monitor or a mobile device. The reason is that different devices have different pixels sizes and so, an image that displays on one device (such as a smartphone) with a certain physical size, might display on other devices (such as an LCD projector) in another size altogether. For the purpose of displaying an image on a screen, you can ignore the resolution parameter. For the same reason, do not use any size unit other than the pixel in the height / width fields.

If you know the desired width, enter it in the dialog at the top where it says Width. This is shown in the figure above. If you don't have such a number in mind, choose an appropriate width for the desired use. Common screen sizes range between 320 pixels for simpler phones, 1024 pixels for a netbook, 1440 for a wide-screen PC display and 1920 pixels for an HD screen. for the purpose of displaying an image on-line, a width of 600 to 800 pixels offers a good compromise.

When you change one of the image's dimensions, GIMP changes the other dimension proportionally. To change the other dimension, see **Section 4.5, "Crop An Image"**. Bear in mind that when you change the two dimensions arbitrarily, the image might become stretched or squashed.

4.3. Change the Size of an Image for print

As discussed before, pixels don't have a set size in the real world. When you set out to print an image on paper, GIMP needs to know how big each pixels is. We use a parameter called resolution to set the ratio between pixels and real-world units such as inches.

By default, most images open with the resolution set to 72. This number was chosen for historical reasons as it was the resolution of screens in the past, and means that when printed, every pixel is 1/72 of an inch wide. When printing images are taken with modern digital cameras, this produces very large but chunky images with visible pixels. What we want to do is tell GIMP to print it with the size we have in mind, but not alter the pixel data so as not to lose quality.

To change the print size use Image → Print Size to open the "Print Size" dialog. Select a size unit you are comfortable with, such as "inches". Set one dimension, and let GIMP change the other one proportionally. Now examine the change in resolution. If the resolution is 300 pixels per Inch or over, the printed image's quality will be very high and pixels will not be noticeable. With a resolution of between 200 and 150 ppi, pixels will be somewhat noticeable, but the image will be fine as long as its not inspected too closely.

Values lower than 100 are visibly coarse and should only be used for material that is seen from a distance, such as signs or large posters.

Figure 3.20. Dialog for Setting Print Size

4.4. Compressing Images

Figure 3.21. Example Image for JPEG Saving

If you have images that take up a large space on disk, you can reduce that space even without changing the image dimensions. The best image compression is achieved by using the JPG format, but even if the image is already in this format, you can usually still make it take up less space, as the JPG format has an adaptive compression scheme that allows saving in varying levels of compression. The trade-off is that the less space an image takes, the more detail from the original image you lose. You should also be aware that repeated saving in the JPG format causes more and more image degradation.

To save you image as a JPG file, therefore, use File → Save As to open the "Save As" dialog.

Figure 3.22. "Save As" Dialog

The dialog opens with the file name already typed in the Name box. If the image is not a JPG image, delete the existing extension and type JPG instead, and GIMP will determine the file type from the file extension. Use the file extension list, circled in the figure above, to see the types supported by GIMP. The supported extensions change depending on your installed libraries. If GIMP complains, or if "JPEG" is grayed out in the Extensions menu, cancel out of everything and step through the **Section 4.7, "Change the Mode"**. Once you have done this, click Save. This opens the "Save as" " JPEG dialog that contains the quality control.

The "Save as JPEG" dialog uses default values that reduce size while retaining good visual quality; this is the safest and quickest thing to do.

Figure 3.23. "Save as JPEG" dialog with poor quality.

Reduce the image Quality to make the image even smaller. Reduced quality degrades the image, so be certain to check "Show preview in image window" to visually gauge the degradation. As shown in the figure above, a Quality setting of 10 produces a very poor quality image that uses very little disk space. The figure below shows a more reasonable image. A quality of 75 produces a reasonable image using much less disk space, which will, in turn, load much faster on a web page. Although the image is somewhat degraded, it is acceptable for the intended purpose.

Figure 3.24. Dialog for Image Saving as JPEG

Finally, here is a comparison of the same picture with varying degrees of compression:

Figure 3.25. Example for High JPEG Compression

Quality: 10; Size: 3.4 KiloBytes   Quality: 40; Size: 9.3 KiloBytes

Figure 3.26. Example for Moderate JPEG Compression

Quality: 70; Size: 15.2 KiloBytes   Quality: 100; Size: 72.6 KiloBytes

4.5. Crop An Image

Figure 3.27. Example Image for Cropping

Source image

Image after cropping

There are many reasons to crop an image; for example, fitting an image to fill a frame, removing a portion of the background to emphasize the subject, etc.

There are two methods to activate the crop tool. Click the ✎ button in the Toolbox, or use Tools → Transform Tools → Crop in the image window. This changes the cursor and allow you to click and drag a rectangular shape. The button in the toolbox is the easiest way to get to any of the tools.

Figure 3.28. Select a Region to Crop

Click on one corner of the desired crop area and drag your mouse to create the crop rectangle. You don't have to be accurate as you can change the exact shape of the rectangle later.

Figure 3.29. Dialog for Cropping

After completing the click and drag motion, a rectangle with special regions is shown on the canvas. As the cursor is moved over the different areas of the selected crop area, the cursor changes. You can then drag the rectangle's corners or edges to change the dimensions of the selected area. As shown in the figure above, as the crop area is resized, the dimensions and ratio are shown in the status bar. See **Section 4.4, "Crop"** for more information on cropping in GIMP. If you would like to crop the image in a specific aspect ratio, such as a square, make sure the tool options are visible (Windows → Dockable

Dialogs → Tool Options). In the Tool Options dockable, check the mark next to Fixed and make sure the drop-down box next to it is set to Aspect Ratio. You can now type the desired aspect ratio on the text box below, such as "1:1". You also have controls to change the aspect from landscape to portrait. After you set the aspect ratio, drag one of the corners of the crop rectangle to update it. The rectangle changes to the chosen ratio, and when you drag it should maintain that ratio.

4.6. Find Info About Your Image

Figure 3.30. Finding Info

When you need to find out information about your image, Use Image → Image Properties to open the "Image Properties" dialog, which contains information about the image size, resolution, mode and much more.

Figure 3.31. "Image Properties" Dialog

4.7. Change the Mode

As with anything else, images come in different kinds and serve different purposes. Sometimes, a small size is important (for web sites) and at other times, retaining a high color depth (e.g., a family portrait) is what you want. GIMP can handle all of this, and more, primarily by converting between three fundamental modes, as seen in this menu. In order to switch your image to one of these modes, you open it and follow that menu and click the mode you want.

Figure 3.32. Dialog for changing the mode

RGB- This is the default mode, used for high-quality images, and able to display millions of colors. This is also the mode for most of your image work including scaling, cropping, and even flipping. In RGB mode, each pixel consists of three different components: R->Red, G->Green, B->Blue. Each of these in turn can have an intensity value of 0-255. What you see at every pixel is an additive combination of these three components.

Indexed- This is the mode usually used when file size is of concern, or when you are working with images with few colors. It involves using a fixed number of colors (256 or less) for the entire image to represent colors. By default, when you change an image to a palleted image, GIMP generates an "optimum palette" to best represent your image.

Figure 3.33. Dialog "Change to Indexed Colors"

As you might expect, since the information needed to represent the color at each pixel is less, the file size is smaller. However, sometimes, there are options in the various menus that are grayed-out for no apparent reason. This usually means that the filter or option cannot be applied when your image is in its current mode. Changing the mode to RGB, as outlined above, should solve this issue. If RGB mode doesn't work either, perhaps the option you're trying requires your layer to have the ability to be transparent. This can be done just as easily via Layer → Transparency → Add Alpha Channel.

Figure 3.34. Add Alpha Channel

Grayscale- Grayscale images have only shades of gray. This mode has some specific uses and takes less space on the hard drive in some formats, but is not recommended for general use as reading it is not supported by many applications.

There is no need to convert an image to a specific mode before saving it in your favorite format, as GIMP is smart enough to properly export the image.

4.8. Flip An Image

Use this option when you need the person in the photo looking in the other direction, or you need the top of the image to be the bottom. Use Tools → Transform Tools → Flip , or use the button on the toolbox. After selecting the flip tool from the toolbox, click inside the canvas. Controls in the Tool Options dockable let you switch between Horizontal and Vertical modes.

Figure 3.35. Dialog "Flip an Image"

After selecting the flip tool from the toolbox, click inside the canvas. The tool flips the image horizontally. Use the options dialog to switch between horizontal and vertical. If it is not already displayed in the dock under the toolbox, double click the toolbox button. You can also use the **Ctrl** key to switch between horizontal and vertical.

In the images below, all possible flips are demonstrated:

Figure 3.36. Example Image to Flip

Source image

Horizontal flipped image

Vertical flipped image

Horizontal and vertical flipped image

4.9. Rotate An Image

Figure 3.37. Menu for "Rotate An Image"

Images that are taken with digital cameras sometimes need to be rotated. To do this, use Image → Transform → Rotate 90° clockwise (or counter-clockwise). The images below demonstrate a 90 degrees CCW rotation.

Figure 3.38. Example for "Rotate An Image"

Source Image   Rotated image 90 degree CCW

4.10. Separating an Object From Its Background

Figure 3.39. Object with Background

Sometimes you need to separate the subject of an image from its background. You may want to have the subject on a flat color, or keep the background transparent so you can use it on an existing background, or any other thing you have in mind. To do this, you must first use GIMP's selection tools to draw a selection around your subject. This is not an easy task, and selecting the correct tool is crucial. You have several tools to accomplish this.

The "Free Select Tool" allows you to draw a border using either freehand or straight lines. Use this when the subject has a relatively simple shape. Read more about this tool here: **Section 2.4, "Free Selection (Lasso)"**

Figure 3.40. Free Select Tool

The "Intelligent Scissors Select Tool" lets you select a freehand border and uses edge-recognition algorithms to better fit the border around the object. Use this when the subject is complex but distinct enough against its current background. Read more about this tool here: **Section 2.7, "Intelligent Scissors"**

Figure 3.41. Intelligent Scissors Select Tool

The "Foreground Select Tool" lets you mark areas as "Foreground" or "Background" and refines the selection automatically. Read more about this tool here: **Section 2.8, "Foreground Select"**

Figure 3.42. Foreground Select Tool

Once you have selected your subject successfully, use Select → Invert. Now, instead of the subject, the background is selected. What you do now depends on what you intended to do with the background.

- To fill the background with a single color:

    Click the foreground color swatch (the top left of the two overlapping colored rectangles) in the toolbox and select the desired color. Next, use **Section 3.4, "Bucket Fill"** to replace the background with your chosen color.

    Figure 3.43. Result of Adding a Plain Color Background

- To make a transparent background:

    Use Layer → Transparence → Add Alpha Channel to add an alpha channel. Next, use Edit Clear or hit the **Del** key on the keyboard to remove the background. Please note that only a small subset of file formats support transparent areas. Your best bet is to save your image as PNG.

Figure 3.44. Result of Adding a Transparent Background

- To make a black-and-white background while keeping the subject in color:

    Use Colors → Desaturate. In the dialog that opens, cycle between the modes and select the best-looking one, then click OK.

Figure 3.45. Result of Desaturating the Background

5. How to Draw Straight Lines

This tutorial is based on Text and images Copyright © 2002 Seth Burgess. The original tutorial can be found in the Internet TUT01.

5.1. Intention

Figure 3.46. Example of straight lines

This tutorial shows you how to draw straight lines with GIMP. Forcing a line to be straight is a convenient way to deal with the imprecision of a mouse or tablet, and to take advantage of the power of a computer to make things look neat and orderly. This tutorial doesn't use Straight Lines for complex tasks; its intended to show how you can use it to create quick and easy straight lines.

1. **Preparations**

   Figure 3.47. Introducing the Shift-key

   The invention called the typewriter introduced the **Shift** Key. You generally have 2 of them on your keyboard. They look something like the figure above. The keys are located on the left and right sides of your keyboard. The mouse was invented by Douglas C. Engelbart in 1970. These come in different varieties, but always have at least one button.

2. **Creating a Blank Drawable**

   Figure 3.48. New image

   First, create a new image. Any size will do. Use File → New to create a new image.

3. **Choose a Tool**

   Figure 3.49. Paint tools in the toolbox

Any of the red-highlighted tools on the above toolbox can do lines.

4. **Create a Starting Point**

   Figure 3.50. Starting point

   Click on the paintbrush in the toolbox. Click in the image where you want a line to start or end. A single dot will appear on the screen. The size of this dot represents the current brush size, which you can change in the Brush Dialog (see **Section 3.2, "Brushes Dialog"**).Now, lets start drawing a line. Hold down the **Shift** key, and keep it down.

5. **Drawing the Line**

   Figure 3.51. Drawing the line

   After you have a starting point and while pressing the **Shift**, you will see a straight line that follows the cursor. Press the first button on the Mouse (the leftmost one usually) and let it go. During that whole "click" of the Mouse button, you need to keep the **Shift** Key held down.

6. **Final**

   Figure 3.52. Final Image

   This is a powerful feature. You can draw straight lines with any of the draw tools. You can even draw more lines at the end of this one. Our last step is to let go of the **Shift** key. And there you have it. Some more examples are shown below. Happy GIMPing!

5.2. Examples

Figure 3.53. Examples I

Check Use color from gradient.

63

Select the Clone tool and set the source to "Maple Leaves" pattern.

Figure 3.54. Examples II

Use Filters → Render → Pattern → Grid to create a grid. Use the Smudge Tool to draw a line with a slightly larger brush.

Use Filters → Render → Clouds → Plasma to create the cool plasma cloud. Use the Erase Tool with a square brush to draw a line.

Figure 3.55. Example III

Use the rectangle select tool to select a rectangle, and then fill the selection with a light blue color. Select the dodge/burn tool. Set the type to Dodge and paint along the top and left side using an appropriately sized brush. Set the type to Burn and paint along the right and bottom.

Chapter 4. Getting Unstuck

1. Getting Unstuck

1.1. Stuck!

All right, okay: you're stuck. You're trying to use one of the tools on an image, and nothing is happening, and nothing you try makes any difference. Your fists are starting to clench, and your face is starting to feel warm. Are you going to have to kill the program, and lose all your work? This sucks!

Well, hold on a second. This happens pretty frequently, even to people who've used GIMP for a long time, but generally the cause is not so hard to figure out (and fix) if you know where to look. Lets be calm, and go through a checklist that will probably get you GIMPing happily again.

1.2. Common Causes of GIMP Non-Responsiveness

1.2.1. There is a floating selection

Figure 4.1. Layers dialog showing a floating selection.

How to tell: If there is a floating selection, many actions are impossible until the floating section is anchored. To check, look at the Layers dialog (making sure it's set to the image you're working on) and see whether the top layer is called "Floating Selection".

How to solve: Either anchor the floating selection, or convert it into an ordinary (non-floating) layer. If you need help on how to do this, see **Floating Selections** .

1.2.2. The selection is hidden

Figure 4.2. Unstuck show selection menu

In the View menu, make sure that "Show Selection" is checked.

How to tell: If this is the problem, merely reading this will already have made you realize it, probably, but to explain in any case: sometimes the flickering line that outlines the selection is annoying because it makes it hard to see important details of the image, so GIMP gives you the option of hiding the selection, by unchecking Show Selection in the View menu. It is easy to forget that you have done this, though.

How to fix: If this hasn't rung any bells, it isn't the problem, and if it has, you probably know how to fix it, because it doesn't happen unless you explicitly tell it to; but anyway: just go to the View menu for the image and, if Show Selection is unchecked, click on it..

1.2.3. You are acting outside of the selection

Figure 4.3. Unstuck select all

```
All                  Ctrl+A
None                 Shift+Ctrl+A
Invert               Ctrl+I
Float                Shift+Ctrl+L
By Color             Shift+O
From Path            Shift+V
Selection Editor

Feather...
Sharpen
Shrink...
Grow...
Border...
Distort...
Rounded Rectangle...

Toggle Quick Mask    Shift+Q
Save to Channel
To Path
```

Click "All" in the Select menu to make sure that everything is selected.

How to fix: If doing this has destroyed a selection that you wanted to keep, hit **Ctrl+Z** (undo) a couple of times to restore it, and then we'll figure out what the problem is. There are a couple of possibilities. If you couldn't see any selection, there may have been a very tiny one, or even one that contained no pixels. If this was the case, it surely is not a selection that you wanted to keep, so why have you gotten this far in the first place? If you can see a selection but thought you were inside it, it might be inverted from what you think. The easiest way to tell is to hit the Quick Mask button: the selected area will be clear and the unselected area will be masked. If this was the problem, then you can solve it by toggling Quick Mask off and choosing Invert in the Select menu.

1.2.4. The active drawable is not visible

Figure 4.4. Unstuck layer invisibility

Layers dialog with visibility off for the active layer.

How to tell: The Layers dialog gives you ability to toggle the visibility of each layer on or off. Look at the Layers dialog, and see if the layer you are trying to act on is active (i.e., darkened) and has an eye symbol to the left of it. If not, this is your problem.

How to fix: If your intended target layer is not active, click on it in the Layers dialog to activate it. (If none of the layers are active, the active drawable might be a channel -- you can look at the Channels tab in the Layers dialog to see. This does not change the solution, though.) If the eye symbol does not appear, click in the Layers dialog at the left edge to toggle it: this should make the layer visible. See the Help section for the **Layers Dialog** if you need more help.

1.2.5. The active drawable is transparent

Figure 4.5. Unstuck layer transparency

Layers dialog with opacity set to zero for the active layer.

How to tell: When the opacity is set 0 on the layer, you cannot see anything which you draw on it. Look the Opacity slider, and see which side the slider placed at. If it is at the leftmost side, that is your problem.

How to fix: Move the slider.

1.2.6. You are trying to act outside the layer

How to tell: In GIMP, layers don't need to have the same dimensions as the image: they can be larger or smaller. If you try to paint outside the borders of a layer, nothing happens. To see if this is happening, look for a black-and-yellow dashed rectangle that does not enclose the area you're trying to draw at.

How to fix: You need to enlarge the layer. There are two commands at the bottom of the Layer menu that will let you do this: Layer to Image Size, which sets the layer bounds to match the image borders; and Layer Boundary Size, which brings up a dialog that allows you to set the layer dimensions to whatever you please.

1.2.7. The image is in indexed color mode.

How to tell: GIMP can handle three different color modes: **RGB(A), Indexed and Grayscale**. The indexed colormode uses a colormap, where all used colors on the image are indexed. The color picker in GIMP however, let you choose RGB colors. That means, if you try to paint with a different color than it is indexed in the colormap, you end up in very undetermined results (e.g. it paints with the wrong color or you can't paint).

How to fix: Always use the RGB Color mode to paint on images. You can verify and select another color mode from the Mode menuitem in the Image menu.

Part II:

How do I Become a GIMP Wizard?

Chapter 5. Getting Images into GIMP

This chapter is about getting images into GIMP. It explains how to create new images, how to load images from files, how to scan them and how to make screenshots.

But first we want to introduce you to the general structure of images in GIMP.

1. Image Types

It is tempting to think of an *image* as something that corresponds with a single display window, or to a single file such as a **JPEG** file. In reality, however, a GIMP image is a complicated structure, containing a stack of layers plus several other types of objects: a selection mask, a set of channels, a set of paths, an "undo" history, etc. In this section we take a detailed look at the components of a GIMP image, and the things that you can do with them.

The most basic property of an image is its *mode*. There are three possible modes: RGB, grayscale, and indexed. RGB stands for Red-Green-Blue, and indicates that each point in the image is represented by a "red" level, a "green" level, and a "blue" level; representing a full-color image. Each color channel has 256 possible intensity levels. More details in **Color Models.**

In a grayscale image, each point is represented by a brightness value, ranging from 0 (black) to 255 (white), with intermediate values representing different levels of gray.

Figure 5.1. Components of the RGB and CMY Color Model

In the RGB Color Model, mixing Red, Green and Blue gives White, which is what happens on your screen.

In the CMY(K) color model, mixing Cyan, Magenta and Yellow gives Black, which is what happens when you print on a white paper. The printer will actually use the black cartridge for economical reasons and better color rendering.

Conceptually, the difference between a grayscale image and an RGB image is the number of "color channels": a grayscale image has one; an RGB image has three. An RGB image can be thought of as three superimposed grayscale images, one colored red, one green, and one blue.

Actually, both RGB and grayscale images have one additional color channel called the *alpha* channel, which represents opacity. When the alpha value at a given location in a given layer is zero, the layer is completely transparent (you can see through it), and the color at that location is determined by what lies underneath. When alpha is maximal (255), the layer is opaque (you cannot see through it), and the color is determined by the color of the layer. Intermediate alpha values correspond to varying degrees of transparency / opacity: the color at the location is a proportional mixture of color from the layer and color from underneath.

Figure 5.2. Example of an image in RGB and Grayscale mode

An image in RGB mode, with the channels corresponding to Red, Green and Blue.

An image in Grayscale mode, with the channel corresponding to Luminosity.

In GIMP, every color channel, including the alpha channel, has a range of possible values from 0 to 255; in computing terminology, a depth of 8 bits. Some digital cameras can produce image files with a depth of 16 bits per color channel. GIMP cannot load such a file without losing resolution. In most cases the effects are too subtle to be detected by the human eye, but in some cases, mainly where there are large areas with slowly varying color gradients, the difference may be perceptible.

Figure 5.3. Example of an image with alpha channel

Red channel   Green channel   Blue channel

The Alpha channel shows the image area which is transparent.

A color image in RGB mode with an Alpha channel.

The third type, *indexed* images, is a bit more complicated to understand. In an indexed image, only a limited set of discrete colors are used, usually 256 or less. These colors form the "colormap" of the image, and each point in the image is assigned a color from the colormap. Indexed images have the advantage that they can be represented inside a computer in a way which consumes relatively little memory, and back in the dark ages (say, ten years ago), they were very commonly used. As time goes on, they are used less and less, but they are still important enough to be worth supporting in GIMP. (Also, there are a few important kinds of image manipulation that are easier to implement with indexed images than with continuous-color RGB images.)

Some very commonly used types of files (including **GIF** and **PNG**) produce indexed images when they are opened in GIMP. Many of GIMP's tools don't work very well on indexed images–and many filters don't work at all–because of the limited number of colors available. Because of this, it is usually best to convert an image to RGB mode before working on it. If necessary, you can convert it back to indexed mode when you are ready to save it

GIMP makes it easy to convert from one image type to another, using the **Mode** command in the Image menu. Some types of conversions, of course (RGB to grayscale or indexed, for example) lose information that cannot be regained by converting back in the other direction.

> **Note**
>
> If you are trying to use a filter on an image, and it appears grayed out in the menu, usually the cause is that the image (or, more specifically, the layer) you are working on is the wrong type. Many filters can't be used on indexed images. Some can be used only on RGB images, or only on grayscale images. Some also require the presence or absence of an alpha channel. Usually the fix is to convert the image to a different type, most commonly RGB.

2. Creating new Files

Use File → New to open the Create a new image dialog. Modify the initial width and height of the file or use the standard values, then create a new image file. More information about the Create a new image dialog can be found in **Section 2.2, "New"**.

3. Opening Files

There are several ways of opening an existing image in GIMP:

3.1. Open File

The most obvious way to open an existing image is the menu. Use File → Open to open the Open Image dialog, allowing you to navigate to the file and click on its name. This method works well if you know the name and location of the file you want to open. Although the Open Image dialog does have a preview pane, it is not convenient (easy) to find an image based on a thumbnail.

> **Note**
>
> While opening a file, GIMP must determine the file type. Unfortunately, the file extension, such as .jpg, is not reliable: file extensions vary from system to system; any file can be renamed to have any extension; and there are many reasons why a file name might lack an extension. GIMP first tries to recognize a file by examining its contents: most of the commonly used file formats have "magic headers" that permit them to be recognized. Only if the magic yields no result does GIMP resort to using the extension.

Figure 5.4. The "Open Image" dialog

GIMP 2.2 introduced a new Open Image dialog that provides several features to help you navigate quickly to a file. Perhaps the most important is the ability to create "bookmarks", or Places, for folders that you use often. Your list of bookmarks appears on the left side of the dialog. The ones at the top, such as "Desktop", are provided automatically. Use the Add button to add the current directory to the list. Use the Remove button to remove the selected bookmark. Double-click on a bookmark to navigate directly to that directory.

The center of the dialog contains a listing of the contents of the selected directory. Subdirectories are shown at the top of the list, files below them. By default, all files in the directory are listed, but you can restrict the listing to image files of a specific type using the File Type selection menu that appears beneath the directory listing.

When you select an image file entry in the listing, a preview appears on the right side of the dialog, along with some basic information about the image. Note that previews are cached when they are generated, and there are some things you can do that may cause a preview to be incorrect. If you suspect that this may be happening, you can force a new preview to be generated by holding down the **Ctrl** key and clicking in the Preview area.

By default, a Location text box is present in the File Open dialog. It may be absent: the **Ctrl+L** key combination toggles this text box. Alternatively, you can click on the icon of the paper and pencil in the upper left corner to toggle the text box.

> **Note**
>
> If you select a file name from the list, and click the "Open" button in the lower right corner or the dialog, it is almost always true that GIMP will automatically determine the file type for you. On rare occasions, mainly if the file type is unusual and the name lacks a meaningful extension, GIMP may fail to correctly identify the file type. Use Select File Type at the bottom of the dialog to manually specify the file type if this is required. More commonly, though, if GIMP fails to open an image file, it is either corrupt or not a supported format.

3.2. Open Location

If instead of a file name, you have a URI (i.e., a web address) for the image, you can open it using the menu, by choosing File → Open Location… from an image menu. This brings up a small dialog that allows you to enter (or paste) the URI.

Figure 5.5. The "Open Location" dialog

The "Open Location" dialog.

3.3. Open Recent

The easiest way to open an image that was recently open in GIMP, may be using File → Open Recent. This displays a scrollable list of the mostly recently opened images with icons beside them. Select and open the desired image.

3.4. Using External Programs

GIMP uses plugins for reading and writing all file formats except XCF. These plugins may use external libraries or programs. For example, GIMP does not directly support **PostScript**. Instead, for reading (or writing) PostScript files (file extension .ps or .eps), GIMP requires a powerful free software program called Ghostscript.

Installing Ghostscript

Linux distributions almost always come with Ghostscript already installed (not necessarily the most recent version). For other operating systems, you may have to install it yourself. Here are instructions for installing it on Windows:

- Go to the Ghostscript project page on Sourceforge **GHOSTSCRIPT**.
- Look for the package gnu-gs or ghostscript (for non-commercial use only) and go to the download section.
- Download one of the prepared Windows distributions, such as gs650w32.exe or gs700w32.exe.
- Start the executable and follow the instructions for the installation procedure.
- Set the GS_PROG environment variable to the full file name of the gswin32c binary (e.g. C:\gs\gsX.YY\bin\gswin32c.exe).

Now you should be able to read PostScript files with GIMP. Please note that you must not move the Ghostscript directories once the installation is complete. The installation creates registry entries which allow Ghostscript to find its libraries. (These instructions courtesy of http://www.kirchgessner.net.)

3.5. File Manager

If you have associated an image file type with GIMP, either when you installed GIMP or later, then you can navigate to the file using a file manager (such as Nautilus or Konqueror in Linux, or Windows Explorer in Windows), and once you have found it, double-click on the file. If properly configured, the image will open in GIMP.

3.6. Drag and Drop

Drag and drop a file onto the GIMP Toolbox to open the file. Drag an image into an open GIMP image to add dropped file as a new layer, or set of layers, to the already open image.

Many applications support dragging and dropping an image into GIMP; for example, drag an image from Firefox and drop it onto GIMP's toolbox.

3.7. Copy and Paste

Use File → Create → From Clipboard to create a new image from the clipboard; alternatively, you can use Edit → Past as → New image. Many applications support copying an image to the clipboard that can then be pasted into GIMP. Many operating systems support copying screens to the clipboard. **Print Screen** typically copies the screen to the clipboard, and **ALT+Print Screen** copies only the active window. Print screen is not universally supported, and just because your operating system can copy an image to the clipboard, does not mean that GIMP can use the image from the clipboard. Your best bet is to try it and see if it works.

3.8. Image Browser

Linux supports an image-management application named gThumb. Besides being an excellent image browser, you can right click an image, choose Open with, then select GIMP from the list of options. You can also drag an image from gThumb onto the GIMP toolbox. See the gThumb home page GTHUMB for more information. Other similar applications are: GQview GQVIEW, and XnView XNVIEW.

Chapter 6. Getting Images out of GIMP

1. Files

GIMP is capable of reading and writing a large variety of graphics file formats. With the exception of GIMP's native XCF file type, file handling is done by Plugins. Thus, it is relatively easy to extend GIMP to support new file types when the need arises.

1.1. Save / Export Images

> **Note**
>
> In former GIMP releases, when you loaded an image in some format, let us say JPG or PNG, the image kept its format and was saved in the same format by **Save**. With GIMP-2.8, images are loaded, imported, in the XCF format as a new project. For example, a "sunflower.png" image will be loaded as "*[sunflower] (imported)-1.0 (indexed color, 1 layer)". The leading asterisk indicates that this file has been changed. This image will be saved as "sunflower.xcf" by **Save**. To save this image in a format other than XCF, you must use **Export**.

When you are finished working with an image, you will want to save the results. (In fact, it is often a good idea to save at intermediate stages too: GIMP is a pretty robust program, but we have heard rumors, possibly apocryphal, that it may have been known on rare and mysterious occasions to crash.) Most of the file formats that GIMP can open, can also be used for saving. There is one file format that is special, though: XCF is GIMP's native format, and is useful because it stores *everything* about an image (well, almost everything; it does not store "undo" information). Thus, the XCF format is especially suitable for saving intermediate results, and for saving images to be re-opened later in GIMP. XCF files are not readable by most other programs that display images, so once you have finished, you will probably also want to export the image in a more widely used format, such as JPEG, PNG, TIFF, etc.

1.2. File Formats

There are several commands for *saving* images. A list, and information on how to use them, can be found in the section covering the **File Menu**.

GIMP allows you to *export* the images you create in a wide variety of formats. It is important to realize that the only format capable of saving *all* of the information in an image, including layers, transparency, etc., is GIMP's native

XCF format. Every other format preserves some image properties and loses others. It is up to you to understand the capabilities of the format you choose.

Exporting an image does not modify the image itself, so you do not lose anything by exporting. See **Export file.**

> **Note**
>
> When you close an image (possibly by quitting GIMP), you are warned if the image is "dirty"; that is, if it has been changed without subsequently being saved (an asterisk is in front of the image name).

Figure 6.1. Closing warning

Saving an image in any file format will cause the image to be considered "not dirty", even if the file format does not represent all of the information from the image.

1.2.1. Export Image as GIF

Figure 6.2. The GIF Export dialog

> **Warning**
>
> The GIF file format does not support some basic image properties such as *print resolution*. If you care for these properties, use a different file format like PNG.

GIF Options

    Interlace

    Checking interlace allows an image on a web page to be progressively displayed as it is downloaded. Progressive image display is useful with slow connection speeds, because you can stop an image that is of no interest; interlace is of less use today with our faster connection speeds.

    GIF comment

    GIF comments support only 7-bit ASCII characters. If you use a character outside the 7-bit ASCII set, GIMP will export the image without a comment, and then inform you that the comment was not saved.

Animated GIF Options

    Loop forever

    When this option is checked, the animation will play repeatedly until you stop it.

    Delay between frames where unspecified

    You can set the delay, in milliseconds, between frames if it has not been set before. In this case, you can modify every delay in the Layer Dialog.

    Frame disposal where unspecified

    If this has not been set before, you can set how frames will be superimposed. You can select among three options :

- I don't care: you can use this option if all your layers are opaque. Layers will overwrite what is beneath.
- Cumulative Layers (combine): previous frames will not be deleted when a new one is displayed.
- One frame per layer (replace): previous frames will be deleted before displaying a new frame.

Use delay entered above for all frames

Self-explanatory.

Use disposal entered above for all frames

Self-explanatory.

1.2.2. Export Image as JPEG

JPEG files usually have an extension .jpg, .JPG, or .jpeg. It is a very widely used format, because it compresses images very efficiently, while minimizing the loss of image quality. No other format comes close to achieving the same level of compression. It does not, however, support transparency or multiple layers.

Figure 6.3. The JPEG Export dialog

The JPEG algorithm is quite complex, and involves a bewildering number of options, whose meaning is beyond the scope of this documentation. Unless you are a JPEG expert, the Quality parameter is probably the only one you will need to adjust.

Quality

When you save a file in JPEG format, a dialog is displayed that allows you to set the Quality level, which ranges from 0 to 100. Values above 95 are generally not useful, though. The default quality of 85 usually produces excellent results, but in many cases it is possible to set the quality substantially lower without noticeably degrading the image. You can test the effect of different quality settings by checking Show Preview in image window in the JPEG dialog.

> **Note**
>
> Please note, that the numbers for the JPEG quality level have a different meaning in different applications. Saving with a quality level of 80 in GIMP is not necessarily comparable with saving with a quality level of 80 in a different application.

Preview in image window

Checking this option causes each change in quality (or any other JPEG parameter) to be shown in the image display. (This does not alter the image: the image reverts back to its original state when the JPEG dialog is closed.)

Advanced settings

Some information about the advanced settings:

Optimize

If you enable this option, the optimization of entropy encoding parameters will be used. The result is typically a smaller file, but it takes more time to generate.

Progressive

With this option enabled, the image chunks are stored in the file in an order that allows progressive image refinement during a slow connection web download. The progressive option for JPG has the same purpose as the interlace option for GIF. Unfortunately, the progressive option produces slightly larger JPG files (than without the progressive option).

Save EXIF data

JPEG files from many digital cameras contain extra information, called EXIF data. EXIF data provides information about the image such as camera make and model, image size, image date, etc. Although GIMP uses the "libexif" library to read and write EXIF data, the library is not automatically packaged with GIMP. If GIMP was built with libexif support, then EXIF data is preserved if you open a JPEG file, work with the resulting image, and then export it as JPEG. The EXIF data is not altered in any way when you do this. The EXIF data may indicate things such as image creation time and file name, which may no longer be correct. If GIMP was not built with EXIF support, you can still open JPG files containing EXIF data, but the EXIF data is ignored, and will not be saved when the resulting image is later exported.

Save thumbnail

This option lets you save a thumbnail with the image. Many applications use the small thumbnail image as a quickly available small preview image.

> **Note**
>
> This option is present only if GIMP was built with EXIF support.

Save XMP data

XMP data is "meta" data about the image; it is a competing format with EXIF. If you enable this option, the meta data of the image is saved in an XMP-structure within the file.

Use quality settings from original image

If a particular quality setting (or "quantization table") was attached to the image when it was loaded, then this option allows you to use them instead of the standard ones.

If you have only made a few changes to the image, then re-using the same quality setting will give you almost the same quality and file size as the original image. This will minimize the losses caused by the quantization step, compared to what would happen if you used different quality setting.

If the quality setting found in the original file are not better than your default quality settings, then the option "Use quality settings from original image" will be available but not enabled. This ensures that you always get at least the minimum quality specified in your defaults. If you did not make major changes to the image and you want to save it using the same quality as the original, then you can do it by enabling this option.

Smoothing

JPG compression creates artifacts. By using this option, you can smooth the image when saving, reducing them. But your image becomes somewhat blurred.

Restart markers

The image file can include markers which allow the image to be loaded as segments. If a connection is broken while loading the image in a web page, loading can resume from the next marker.

Subsampling

The human eye is not sensitive in the same way over the entire color spectrum. The compression can use this to treat slightly different colors that the eye perceives as very close, as identical colors. Three methods are available :

- 1x1,1x1,1x1 (best quality): Commonly referred to as (4:4:4), this produces the best quality, preserving borders and contrasting colors, but compression is less.
- 2x1,1x1,1x1 (4:2:2): This is the standard subsampling, which usually provides a good ratio between image quality and file size. There are situations, however, in which using no subsampling (4:4:4) provides a noticeable increase in the image quality; for example, when the image contains fine details such as text over a uniform background, or images with almost-flat colors.
- 1x2,1x1,1x1 This is similar to (2x1,1x1,1x1), but the chroma sampling is in the horizontal direction rather than the vertical direction; as if someone rotated an image.
- 2x2,1x1,1x1 (smallest file): Commonly referred to as (4:1:1), this produces the smallest files. This suits images with weak borders but tends to denature colors.

DCT Method

DCT is "discrete cosine transform", and it is the first step in the JPEG algorithm going from the spatial to the frequency domain. The choices are "float", "integer" (the default), and "fast integer".

- float: The float method is very slightly more accurate than the integer method, but is much slower unless your machine has very fast floating-point hardware. Also note that the results of the floating-point method may vary slightly across machines,

while the integer methods should give the same results everywhere.
- integer (the default): This method is faster than "float", but not as accurate.
- fast integer: The fast integer method is much less accurate than the other two.

Image comments

In this text box, you can enter a comment which is saved with the image.

1.2.3. Export Image as PNG

Figure 6.4. The "Export Image as PNG" dialog

Interlacing

Checking interlace allows an image on a web page to be progressively displayed as it is downloaded. Progressive image display is useful with slow connection speeds, because you can stop an image that is of no interest; interlace is of less use today with our faster connection speeds.

Save background color

> If your image has many transparency levels, the Internet browsers that recognize only two levels, will use the background color of your Toolbox instead. Internet Explorer up to version 6 did not use this information.

Save gamma

> Gamma correction is the ability to correct for differences in how computers interpret color values. This saves gamma information in the PNG that reflects the current Gamma factor for your display. Viewers on other computers can then compensate to ensure that the image is not too dark or too bright.

Save layer offset

> PNG supports an offset value called the "oFFs chunk", which provides position data. Unfortunately, PNG offset support in GIMP is broken, or at least is not compatible with other applications, and has been for a long time. Do not enable offsets, let GIMP flatten the layers before saving, and you will have no problems.

Save Resolution

> Save the image resolution, in ppi (pixels per inch).

Save creation time

> Date the file was saved.

Save comment

> You can read this comment in the **Image Properties.**

Save color values from transparent pixels

> With this option is checked, the color values are saved even if the pixels are completely transparent.

Compression level

> Since compression is not lossy, the only reason to use a compression level less than 9, is if it takes too long to compress a file on a slow computer. Nothing to fear from decompression: it is as quick whatever the compression level.

Save Defaults

> Click to save the current settings. Latter, you can use Load Defaults to load the saved settings.

Note

The PNG format supports indexed images. Using fewer colors, therefore, results in a smaller file; this is especially useful for creating web images; see **Section 6.6, "Indexed mode"**.

Computers work on 8 bits blocks named "Byte". A byte allows 256 colors. Reducing the number of colors below 256 is not useful: a byte will be used anyway and the file size will not be less. More, this "PNG8" format, like GIF, uses only one bit for transparency; only two transparency levels are possible, transparent or opaque.

If you want PNG transparency to be fully displayed by Internet Explorer, you can use the AlphaImageLoader DirectX filter in the code of your Web page. See Microsoft Knowledge Base **MSKB-294714**. Please note, that this is not necessary for InternetExplorer 7 and above.

1.2.4. Export Image as TIFF

Figure 6.5. The TIFF Export dialog

Compression

> This option allows you to specify the algorithm used to compress the image.
>
> - None: is fast, and lossless, but the resulting file is very large.
> - LZW: The image is compressed using the "Lempel-Ziv-Welch" algorithm, a lossless compression technique. This is old, but efficient and fast. More information at **WKPD-LZW** .
> - Pack Bits: is a fast, simple compression scheme for run-length encoding of data. Apple introduced the PackBits format with the release of MacPaint on the Macintosh computer. A PackBits data stream consists of packets of one byte of header followed by data. (Source: WKPD-PACKBITS)
> - Deflate: is a lossless data compression algorithm that uses a combination of the LZ77 algorithm and Huffman coding. It is also used in Zip, Gzip and PNG file formats. Source: WKPD-DEFLATE.
> - JPEG: is a very good compression algorithm but lossy.
> - CCITT Group 3 fax; CCITT Group 4 fax is a black and white format developed to transfer images by FAX.
>
> **Note**
>
> These options can only be selected, if the image is in indexed mode and reduced to two colors. Use Image → Mode → Indexed to convert the image to indexed. Be certain to check "Use black and white (1-bit) palette".

Save color values from transparent pixels

> With this option the color values are saved even if the pixels are completely transparent.

Comment

> In this text box, you can enter a comment that is associated with the image.

1.2.5. Export Image as MNG

Figure 6.6. Export MNG File Dialog

90

MNG is acronym for "Multiple-Image Network Graphics".

The main problem is that Konqueror is the only Web navigator that recognizes the MNG animation format.

2. Preparing your Images for the Web

One of the most common uses for GIMP, is to prepare images for web sites. This means that images should look as nice as possible while keeping the file size as small as possible. This step-by-step guide demonstrates how to create small files with minimal loss of image quality.

2.1. Images with an Optimal Size/Quality Ratio

An optimal image for the web depends upon the image type and the file format. Use **JPEG** for Photographs because they usually have many colors and great detail. An image with fewer colors, such as a button, icon, or screenshot, is better suited to the **PNG** format.

1. First, open the image as usual. I have opened our Wilber as an example image.

   Figure 6.7. The Wilber image opened in RGBA mode

2. The image is now in RGB mode, with an additional **Alpha channel** (RGBA). There is usually no need to have an alpha channel for your web image. You can remove the alpha channel by flattening the image.

   A photograph rarely has an alpha channel, so the image will open in RGB mode rather than RGBA mode; and you won't have to remove the alpha channel.

   > **Note**
   >
   > If the image has a soft transition into the transparent areas, you should not remove the alpha channel, since the information used for the transition is not be saved in the file. To export an image with transparent areas that do not have a soft transition, (similar to **GIF**), remove the alpha channel.

3. After you have flattened the image, export the image in the PNG format for your web site.

   > **Note**
   >
   > You can export your image in the PNG format with the default settings. Always using maximum compression when creating the

image. Maximum compression has no affect on image quality or the time required to display the image, but it does take longer to export. A JPEG image, however, loses quality as the compression is increased. If your image is a photograph with lots of colors, you should use jpeg. The main thing is to find the best tradeoff between quality and compression. You can find more information about this topic in **Section 1.2.2, "Export Image as JPEG"**.

2.2. Reducing the File Size Even More

If you want to reduce the size of your image a bit more, you could convert your image to Indexed mode. That means that all of the colors will be reduced to only 256 values. Do not convert images with smooth color transitions or gradients to indexed mode, because the original smooth gradients are typically converted into a series of bands. Indexed mode is not recommended for photographs because after the conversion, they typically look coarse and grainy.

Figure 6.8. The indexed image

An indexed image can look a bit grainy. The left image is Wilber in its original size, the right image is zoomed in by 300 percent.

1. Use the command described in **Section 6.3, "Mode"** to convert an RGB image to indexed mode.
2. After you convert an image to indexed mode, you are once again able to export the image in **PNG format**.

2.3. Saving Images with Transparency

There are two different approaches used by graphic file formats for supporting transparent image areas: simple binary transparency and alpha transparency. Simple binary transparency is supported in the **GIF** format; one color from the indexed color palette is marked as the transparent color. Alpha transparency is supported in the **PNG** format; the transparency information is stored in a separate channel, the **Alpha channel.**

> **Note**
>
> The GIF format is rarely used because PNG supports all the features of GIF with additional features (e.g., alpha transparency). Nevertheless, GIF is still used for animations.

Procedure 6.1. Creating an Image with Transparent Areas (Alpha Transparency)

1. First of all, we will use the same image as in the previous tutorials, Wilber the GIMP mascot.

Figure 6.9. The Wilber image opened in RGBA mode

2. To export an image with alpha transparency, you must have an alpha channel. To check if the image has an alpha channel, go to the **channel dialog** and verify that an entry for "Alpha" exists, besides Red, Green and Blue. If this is not the case, **add a new alpha channel** from the layers menu; Layer+Transparency → Add Alpha Channel.
3. The original XCF file contains background layers that you can remove. GIMP comes with standard filters that supports creating gradients; look under Filters+Light and Shadow. You are only limited by your imagination. To demonstrate the capabilities of alpha transparency, a soft glow in the background around Wilber is shown.
4. After you're done with your image, you can **export** it in **PNG format**.

Figure 6.10. The Wilber image with transparency

Mid-Tone Checks in the background layer represent the transparent region of the exported image while you are working on it in GIMP.

Chapter 7. Painting with GIMP

1. The Selection

Often when you operate on an image, you only want part of it to be affected. In GIMP, you make this happen by *selecting* that part. Each image has a *selection* associated with it. Most, but not all, GIMP operations act only on the selected portions of the image.

Figure 7.1. How would you isolate the tree?

There are many, many situations where creating just the right selection is the key to getting the result you want, and often it is not easy to do. For example, in the above image, suppose I want to cut the tree out from its background, and paste it into a different image. To do this, I need to create a selection that contains the tree and nothing but the tree. It is difficult because the tree has a complex shape, and in several spots is hard to distinguish from the objects behind it.

Figure 7.2. Selection shown as usual with dashed line.

Now here is a very important point, and it is crucial to understand this. Ordinarily when you create a selection, you see it as a dashed line enclosing a portion of the image. The common, not entirely accurate, idea you could get from this, is that the selection is a sort of container, with the selected parts of the image inside, and the unselected parts outside. Although this concept of selection is okay for many purposes, it is not entirely correct.

Actually the selection is implemented as a *channel*. In terms of its internal structure, it is identical to the red, green, blue, and alpha channels of an image. Thus, the selection has a value defined at each pixel of the image, ranging between 0 (unselected) and 255 (fully selected). The advantage of this approach is that it allows some pixels to be *partially selected*, by giving them intermediate values between 0 and 255. As you will see, there are many situations where it is desirable to have smooth transitions between selected and unselected regions.

What, then, is the dashed line that appears when you create a selection?

The dashed line is a *contour line*, dividing areas that are more than half selected from areas that are less than half selected.

Figure 7.3. Same selection in QuickMask mode.

While looking at the dashed line that represents the selection, always remember that the line tells only part of the story. If you want to see the selection in complete detail, the easiest way is to click the QuickMask button in the lower left corner of the image window. This causes the selection to be shown as a translucent overlay atop the image. Selected areas are unaffected; unselected areas are reddened. The more completely selected an area is, the less red it appears.

Many operations work differently in QuickMask mode, as mentioned in the **QuickMask overview**. Use the QuickMask button in the lower left corner of the image window to toggle QuickMask mode on and off.

Figure 7.4. Same selection in QuickMask mode after feathering.

1.1. Feathering

With the default settings, the basic selection tools, such as the Rectangle Select tool, create sharp selections. Pixels inside the dashed line are fully selected, and pixels outside completely unselected. You can verify this by toggling QuickMask: you see a clear rectangle with sharp edges, surrounded by uniform red. Use the "Feather edges" checkbox in the Tool Options to toggle between graduated selections and sharp selections. The feather radius, which you can adjust, determines the distance over which the transition occurs.

If you are following along, try this with the Rectangle Select tool, and then toggle QuickMask. You will see that the clear rectangle has a fuzzy edge.

Feathering is particularly useful when you are cutting and pasting, so that the pasted object blends smoothly and unobtrusively with its surroundings.

It is possible to feather a selection at any time, even if it was originally created as a sharp selection. Use Select → Feather from the image menu to open the Feather Selection dialog. Set the feather radius and click OK. Use Select → Sharpen to do the opposite—sharpen a graduated selection into an all-or-nothing selection.

> **Note**
>
> For technically oriented readers: feathering works by applying a Gaussian blur to the selection channel, with the specified blurring radius.

1.2. Making a Selection Partially Transparent

You can set layer opacity, but you cannot do that directly for a selection. It is quite useful to make the image of a glass transparent. Use the following methods to set the layer opacity:

- For simple selections, use the Eraser tool with the desired opacity.
- For complex selections: use Selection → Floating to create a floating selection. This creates a new layer with the selection called "Floating Selection". Set the opacity slider in the Layer Dialog to the desired opacity. Then anchor the selection: outside the selection, the mouse pointer includes an anchor. When you click while the mouse pointer includes the anchor, the floating selection disappears from the Layer Dialog and the selection is at the right place and partially transparent (anchoring works this way only if a selection tool is activated : you can also use the Anchor Layer command in the context menu by right clicking on the selected layer in the layer dialog).

  And, if you use this function frequently: **Ctrl-C** to copy the selection, **Ctrl-V** to paste the clipboard as a floating selection, and Layer → New Layer to turn the selection into a new layer. You can adjust the opacity before, or after creating the new layer.

- Another way: use Layer → Mask → Add Layer Mask to add a layer mask to the layer with the selection, initializing it with the selection. Then use a brush with the desired opacity to paint the selection with black, i.e. paint it with transparency. Then Layer/Mask/Apply Layer Mask. See **Section 2.1.3, "Layer masks"**.
- To *make the solid background of an image transparent*, add an Alpha channel, and use the Magic Wand to select the background. Then, use the Color Picker tool to select the background color, which becomes the foreground color in Toolbox. Use the Bucket Fill tool with the selected color. Set the Bucket Fill mode to "Color Erase", which erases pixels with the selected color; other pixels are partially erased and their color is changed.

  The simplest method is to use Edit → Clear, which gives complete transparency to a selection.

2. Creating and Using Selections

2.1. Moving a Selection

Rectangular and elliptical selections have two modes. The default mode has handles on the selection. If you click the selection or press the **Enter** key, the handles disappear leaving only the dotted outline (marching ants). The other selection tools have different behaviour.

2.1.1. Moving rectangular and elliptical selections

If you click-and-drag a selection with handles, you move the selection outline, and you don't move the contents of rectangular or elliptic selections.

Select the **Move** tool and set the options to move the selection; the tool supports moving the selection, path, or layer.

Figure 7.5. Moving selection outline

Most systems support moving the selection using the arrow keys. The precise behavior is system dependent. If the arrow keys do not cause the selection to move, try hovering the mouse cursor over the selection first. Press and hold the **Alt** (or **Ctrl+Alt**, **Shift+Alt**, or **Alt**). One combination may move the selection by one pixel, and another by 25 pixels each step. Hover the mouse cursor over a side or corner handle, and the arrow keys and combinations can change the size of the selection.

If you click-and-drag the selection without handles, you create a new selection! To move the selection contents, you have to

- hold down **Ctrl+Alt** keys and click-and-drag the selection. This makes the original place empty. A floating selection is created. The required key commands may differ on your system, look in the status bar to see if another combination is specified; for example, **Shift+Ctrl+Alt**.

Figure 7.6. Moving a selection and its content, emptying the original place

- hold down **Shift**+**Alt** keys and click-and-drag the selection to move without emptying the original place. A floating selection is created.

Figure 7.7. Moving a selection and its content without emptying the original place

Note

On some systems, you must push **Alt** before **Shift** or **Ctrl**. On these systems, pressing **Shift** or **Ctrl** first, causes GIMP to enter a mode that adds or subtract from the current selection — after that, the **Alt** key is ineffective!

2.1.2. *Moving the other selections*

The other selections (Lasso, Magic wand, By Color) have no handle. Click-and dragging them doesn't move them. To move their contents, as with rectangular and elliptical selections, you have to hold down **Ctrl**+**Alt** keys or **Shift**+**Alt** and click-and-drag.

If you use keyboard arrow keys instead of click-and-drag, you move the outline.

2.1.3. *Other method*

Note

You can also use a more roundabout method to move a selection. Make it floating. Then you can move its content, emptying the origin, by click-and-dragging or keyboard arrow keys. To move without emptying, use copy-paste.

2.2. Adding or subtracting selections

Tools have options that you can configure. Each selection tool allows you to set the selection mode. The following selection modes are supported:

- Replace is the most used selection mode. In replace mode, a selection replaces any existing selection.
- Add mode, causes new selections to be added to any existing selection. Press and hold the **Shift** key while making a selection to temporarily enter add mode.
- Subtract mode, causes new selections to be removed from any existing selection. Press and hold the **Ctrl** key while making a selection to temporarily enter subtract mode.
- Intersect mode, causes areas in both the new and existing selection to become the new selection. Press and hold both the **Shift** and **Ctrl** key while making a selection to temporarily enter intersect mode.

Figure 7.8. Enlarging a rectangular selection with the Lasso

The figure shows an existing rectangular selection. Select the Lasso. While pressing the **Shift** key, make a free hand selection that includes the existing selection. Release the mouse button and areas are included in the selection.

> **Note**
>
> To correct selection defects precisely, use the **Quick Mask**.

3. The QuickMask

Figure 7.9. Image with QuickMask enabled

The usual **selection tools** involve tracing an outline around an area of interest, which does not work well for some complex selections. The QuickMask, however, allows you to paint a selection instead of just tracing its outline.

3.1. Overview

Normally, a selection in GIMP is represented by "marching ants" that trace the selection outline, but there may be more to a selection than the marching ants show. A GIMP selection is actually a full-fledged grayscale channel, covering the image, with pixel values ranging from 0 (unselected) to 255 (fully selected). The marching ants are drawn along a contour of half-selected pixels. Thus, what the marching ants show you as either inside or outside the boundary is really just a slice through a continuum.

The QuickMask is GIMP's way of showing the full structure of the selection. QuickMask also provides the ability to interact with the selection in new, and substantially more powerful, ways. Click the small outlined button at the lower left of the image window to toggle QuickMask on and off. The button switches between QuickMask mode, and marching ants mode. You can also use Select → Toggle QuickMask, or **Shift**+**Q**, to toggle between QuickMask and marching ants mode.

In QuickMask mode, the selection is shown as a translucent screen overlying the image, whose transparency at each pixel indicates the degree to which that pixel is selected. By default the mask is shown in red, but you can change this if another mask color is more convenient. The less a pixel is selected, the more it is obscured by the mask. Fully selected pixels are shown completely clear.

In QuickMask mode, many image manipulations act on the selection channel rather than the image itself. This includes, in particular, paint tools. Painting with white selects pixels, and painting with black unselects pixels. You can use any of the paint tools, as well as the bucket fill and gradient fill tools, in this way. Advanced users of GIMP learn that "painting the selection" is the easiest and most effective way to delicately manipulate the image.

> **Tip**
>
> To save a QuickMask selection to a new channel; Make sure that there is a selection and that QuickMask mode is not active in the image window. Use Select → Save to Channel. to create a new channel in the channel dialog called "SelectionMask copy" (repeating this command creates "..copy#1", "...copy#2" and so on...).

> **Tip**
>
> In QuickMask mode, Cut and Paste act on the selection rather than the image. You can sometimes make use of this as the most convenient way of transferring a selection from one image to another.

You can learn more on Selection masks in the section dedicated to the channel dialog.

3.2. Properties

There are two QuickMask properties you can change by right-clicking on the QuickMask button.

- Normally the QuickMask shows unselected areas "fogged over " and selected areas "in clear", but you can reverse this by choosing "Mask Selected Areas" instead of the default "Mask Unselected Areas".
- Use "Configure Color and Opacity" to open a dialog that allows you to set these to values other than the defaults, which are red at 50% opacity.

4. Using QuickMask Mode

1. Open an image or begin a new document.
2. Activate QuickMask mode using the left-bottom button in the image window. If a selection is present the mask is initialized with the content of the selection.
3. Choose any drawing tool. Paint on the QuickMask with black to remove selected areas, and paint with white to add selected areas. Use grey colors to partially select areas.

   You can also use selection tools and fill these selections with the Bucket Fill tool; this does not destroy the QuickMask selections!

4. Toggle QuickMask mode off using the left-bottom button in the image window: the selection will be displayed with marching ants.

5. Paths

Paths are curves (known as Bézier-curves). Paths are easy to learn and use in GIMP. To understand their concepts and mechanism, look at the glossary Bézier-curve or Wikipedia WKPD-BEZIER. The Paths tool is very powerful, allowing you to design sophisticated forms. To use the Paths tool in GIMP, you must first create a path, and then stroke the path.

In GIMP, the term "Stroke path" means to apply a specific style to the path (color, width, pattern...).

A Path has two main purposes:

- You can convert a closed path to a selection.
- Any path, open or closed, can be *stroked*; that is, painted on the image in a variety of ways.

Figure 7.10. Illustration of four different path creating

Four examples of GIMP paths: one closed and polygonal; one open and polygonal; one closed and curved; one with a mixture of straight and curved segments.

5.1. Path Creation

Start by drawing the outline for your path; the outline can be modified later (see the **Paths** tool). To start, select the Paths tool using one of the following methods:

- Use Tools → Path from the image menu.
- Use the relevant icon in toolbox.
- Use the hotkey **B**.

When the Paths tool is selected, the mouse cursor changes into a pointer (arrow) with a curve. Left click in the image to create the first point on the path. Move the mouse to a new point and left click the mouse to create another point linked to the previous point. Although you can create as many points as you desire, you only need two points to learn about Paths. While adding points, the mouse cursor has a little "+" next to the curve, which indicates that clicking will add a new point. When the mouse cursor is close to a line segment, the "+" changes into a cross with arrows; like the move tool.

Move the mouse cursor close to a line segment, left-click and drag the line segment. Two events occur.

- The line segment bends and curves as it is pulled.
- Each line segment has a start point and an end point that is clearly labeled. A "direction line" now projects from each end point for the line segment that was moved.

The curved line segment leaves an end point in the same direction that the "direction line" leaves the end point. The length of the "direction line" controls how far the line segment projects along the "direction line" before curving toward the other end point. Each "direction line" has an empty square box (called a handle) on one end. Click and drag a handle to change the direction and length of a "direction line".

Figure 7.11. Appearance of a path while it is manipulated

Appearance of a path while it is manipulated using the Path tool.

The path is comprised of two components with both straight and curved segments. Black squares are anchor points, the open circle indicates the selected anchor, and the two open squares are the handles associated with the selected anchor.

5.2. Path Properties

Paths, like layers and channels, are components of an image. When an image is saved in GIMP's native XCF file format, any paths it has are saved with it. The list of paths in an image can be viewed and operated on using the **Paths dialog.** You can move a path from one image to another by copying and pasting using the pop-up menu in the Paths dialog, or by dragging an icon from the Paths dialog into the destination image window.

GIMP paths belong to a mathematical type called "Bezier paths". What this means in practical terms is that they are defined by *anchors* and *handles*. "Anchors" are points the path goes through. "Handles" define the direction of a path when it enters or leaves an anchor point: each anchor point has two handles attached to it.

Paths can be very complex. If you create them by hand using the Path tool, unless you are obsessive they probably won't contain more than a few dozen anchor points (often many fewer); but if you create them by transforming a selection into a path, or by transforming text into a path, the result can easily contain hundreds of anchor points, or even thousands.

A path may contain multiple *components*. A "component" is a part of a path whose anchor points are all connected to each other by path segments. The ability to have multiple components in paths allows you to convert them into selections having multiple disconnected parts.

Each component of a path can be either *open* or *closed*: "closed" means that the last anchor point is connected to the first anchor point. If you transform a path into a selection, any open components are automatically converted into closed components by connecting the last anchor point to the first anchor point with a straight line.

Path segments can be either straight or curved. A path is called "polygonal" if all of its segments are straight. A new path segment is always created straight; the handles for the anchor points are directly on top of the anchor points, yielding handles of zero length, which produces straight-line segments. Drag a handle handle away from an anchor point to cause a segment to curve.

One nice thing about paths is that they use very few resources, especially in comparison with images. Representing a path in RAM requires storing only the coordinates of its anchors and handles: 1K of memory is enough to hold a complex path, but not enough to hold a small 20x20 pixel RGB layer. Therefore, it is possible to have literally hundreds of paths in an image without causing any significant stress to your system; the amount of stress that hundreds of paths might cause *you*, however, is another question. Even a path with thousands of segments consumes minimal resources in comparison to a typical layer or channel.

Paths can be created and manipulated using the **Path tool.**

5.3. Paths and Selections

GIMP lets you transform the selection for an image into a path; it also lets you transform paths into selections. For information about the selection and how it works, see the **Selection** section.

When you transform a selection into a path, the path closely follows the "marching ants". Now, the selection is a two-dimensional entity, but a path is a one-dimensional entity, so there is no way to transform the selection into a path without losing information. In fact, any information about partially selected areas (i.e., feathering) are lost when a selection is turned into a path. If the path is transformed back into a selection, the result is an all-or-none selection, similar to what is obtained by executing "Sharpen" from the Select menu.

5.4. Transforming Paths

Each of the Transform tools (Rotate, Scale, Perspective, etc) can be set to act on a layer, selection, or path. Select the transform tool in the toolbox, then select layer, selection, or path for the "Transform:" option in the tool's Tool Options dialog. This gives you a powerful set of methods for altering the shapes of paths without affecting other elements of the image.

By default a Transform tool, when it is set to affect paths, acts on only one path: the *active path* for the image, which is shown highlighted in the Paths dialog. You can make a transformation affect more than one path, and possibly other things as well, using the "transform lock" buttons in the Paths dialog. Not only paths, but also layers and channels, can be transform-locked. If you transform one element that is transform-locked, all others will be transformed in the same way. So, for example, if you want to scale a layer and a path by the same amount, click the transform-lock buttons so that "chain" symbols appear next to the layer in the Layers dialog, and the path in the Paths dialog; then use the Scale tool on either the layer or the path, and the other will automatically follow.

5.5. Stroking a Path

Figure 7.12. Stroking paths

The four paths from the top illustration, each stroked in a different way.

Paths do not alter the appearance of the image pixel data unless they are *stroked*, using Edit → Stroke Path from the image menu or the Paths dialog right-click menu, or the "Stroke Path" button in the Tool Options dialog for the Path tool.

Choosing "Stroke Path" by any of these means brings up a dialog that allows you to control the way the stroking is done. You can choose from a wide variety of line styles, or you can stroke with any of the Paint tools, including unusual ones such as the Clone tool, Smudge tool, Eraser, etc.

7.13. The Stroke Path dialog

You can further increase the range of stroking effects by stroking a path multiple times, or by using lines or brushes of different widths. The possibilities for getting interesting effects in this way are almost unlimited.

5.6. Paths and Text

Figure 7.14. Text converted to a path

Text converted to a path and then transformed using the Perspective tool.

The path shown above, stroked with a fuzzy brush and then gradient-mapped using the Gradient Map filter with the "Yellow Contrast" gradient.

A text item created using the Text tool can be transformed into a path using the **Path from Text** command in the the context menu of the Text tool. This can be useful for several purposes, including:

- Stroking the path, which gives you many possibilities for fancy text.
- More importantly, transforming the text. Converting text into a path, then transforming the path, and finally either stroking the path or converting it to a selection and filling it, often leads to much higher-quality results than rendering the text as a layer and transforming the pixel data.

5.7. Paths and SVG files

SVG, standing for "Scalable Vector Graphics", is an increasingly popular file format for *vector graphics*, in which graphical elements are represented in a resolution-independent format, in contrast to *raster graphics*; in which graphical elements are represented as arrays of pixels. GIMP is mainly a raster graphics program, but paths are vector entities.

Fortunately, paths are represented in SVG files in almost exactly the same way they are represented in GIMP. (Actually fortune has nothing to do with it: GIMP's path handling was rewritten for GIMP 2.0 with SVG paths in mind.)

This compatibility makes it possible to store GIMP paths as SVG files without losing any information. You can access this capability in the Paths dialog.

It also means that GIMP can create paths from SVG files saved in other programs, such as Inkscape or Sodipodi, two popular open-source vector graphics applications. This is nice because those programs have much more powerful path-manipulation tools than GIMP does. You can import a path from an SVG file using the Paths dialog.

The SVG format handles many other graphical elements than just paths: among other things, it handles figures such as squares, rectangles, circles, ellipses, regular polygons, etc. GIMP cannot do anything with these entities, but it can load them as paths.

6. Brushes

Figure 7.15. Brush strokes example

A number of examples of brushstrokes painted using different brushes from the set supplied with GIMP. All were painted using the Paintbrush tool.

A *brush* is a pixmap or set of pixmaps used for painting. GIMP includes a set of 10 "paint tools", which not only perform operations that you would normally think of as painting, but also operations such as erasing, copying, smudging, lightening or darkening, etc. All of the paint tools, except the ink tool, use the same set of brushes. The brush pixmaps represent the marks that are made by single "touches" of the brush to the image. A brush stroke, usually made by moving the pointer across the image with the mouse button held down, produces a series of marks spaced along the trajectory, in a way specified by the characteristics of the brush and the paint tool being used.

Brushes can be selected by clicking on an icon in the **Brushes dialog**. GIMP's *current brush* is shown in the Brush/Pattern/Gradient area of the Toolbox. Clicking on the brush symbol there is one way of activating the Brushes dialog.

When you install GIMP, it comes with a number of basic brushes, plus a few bizarre ones that serve mainly to give you examples of what is possible (i. e., the "green pepper" brush in the illustration). You can also create new brushes, or download them and install them so that GIMP will recognize them.

GIMP can use several different types of brushes. All of them, however, are used in the same way, and for most purposes you don't need to worry about the differences when you paint with them. Here are the available types of brushes:

Ordinary brushes

> Most of the brushes supplied with GIMP fall into this category. They are represented in the Brushes dialog by grayscale pixmaps. When you paint using them, the current foreground color (as shown in the Color Area of the Toolbox) is substituted for black, and the pixmap shown in the brushes dialog represents the mark that the brush makes on the image.
>
> To create such a brush: Create a small image in gray levels using zoom. Save it with the .gbr extension. Click on Refresh button in the Brush Dialog to get it in preview without it being necessary to restart GIMP.

Color brushes

> Brushes in this category are represented by colored images in the Brushes dialog. They can be pictures or text. When you paint with them, the colors are used as shown; the current foreground color does not come into play. Otherwise they work the same way as ordinary brushes.
>
> To create such a brush: Create a small RGBA image. For this, open New Image, select RGB for image type and Transparent for fill type. Draw your image and and firs save it as a .xcf file to keep its properties. Then save it in *.gbr* format. Click on the *Refresh* button in Brush Dialog to get your brush without it being necessary to restart GIMP.

> **Tip**
>
> When you do a Copy or a Cut on a selection, you see the contents of the clipboard (that is the selection) at the first position in the brushes dialog. And you can use it for painting.

Figure 7.16. Selection to Brush after Copy or Cut

Image hoses / Image pipes

> Brushes in this category can make more than one kind of mark on an image. They are indicated by small red triangles at the lower right corner of the brush symbol in the Brushes dialog. They are sometimes called "animated brushes" because the marks change as you trace out a brushstroke. In principle, image hose brushes can be very sophisticated, especially if you use a tablet, changing shape as a function of pressure, angle, etc. These possibilities have never really been exploited, however; and the ones supplied with GIMP are relatively simple (but still quite useful).
>
> You will find an example on how to create such brushes in **Animated brushes.**

Parametric brushes

> These are brushes created using the **Brush Editor**, which allows you to generate a wide variety of brush shapes by using a simple graphical interface. A nice feature of parametric brushes is that they are *resizable*. It is possible, using the Preferences dialog, to make key presses or mouse wheel rotations cause the current brush to become larger or smaller, if it is a parametric brush.

Now, all brushes have a variable size. In fact, in the option box of all painting tools there is a slider to enlarge or reduce the size of the active brush. You can do this directly in the image window if you have set correctly your mouse wheel; see **Varying brush size**.

In addition to the brush pixmap, each GIMP brush has one other important property: the brush *Spacing*. This represents the distance between consecutive brush-marks when a continuous brushstroke is painted. Each brush has an assigned default value for this, which can be modified using the Brushes dialog.

7. Adding New Brushes

To add a new brush, after either creating or downloading it, you need to save it in a format GIMP can use. The brush file needs to be placed in the GIMP's brush search path, so that GIMP is able to index and display it in the Brushes dialog. You can hit the Refresh button, which reindexes the brush directory. GIMP uses three file formats for brushes:

GBR

> The .gbr ("*gimp br*ush") format is used for ordinary and color brushes. You can convert many other types of images, including many brushes used by other programs, into GIMP brushes by opening them in GIMP and saving them with file names ending in .gbr. This brings up a dialog box in which you can set the default Spacing for the brush. A more complete description of the GBR file format can be found in the file gbr.txt in the devel-docs directory of the GIMP source distribution.
>
> **Figure 7.17. Save a .gbr brush**

GIH

> The .gih ("*gimp i*mage *h*ose") format is used for animated brushes. These brushes are constructed from images containing multiple layers: each layer may contain multiple brush-shapes, arranged in a grid. When you save an image as a .gih file, a dialog comes up that allows you to describe the format of the brush. Look at **The GIH dialog box** for more information about the dialog. The GIH format is rather complicated: a complete description can be found in the file gih.txt in the devel-docs directory of the GIMP source distribution.

VBR

> The .vbr format is used for parametric brushes, i. e., brushes created using the Brush Editor. There is really no other meaningful way of obtaining files in this format.

To make a brush available, place it in one of the folders in GIMP's brush search path. By default, the brush search path includes two folders, the system brushes folder, which you should not use or alter, and the brushes folder inside your personal GIMP directory. You can add new folders to the brush search path using the **Brush Folders** page of the Preferences dialog. Any GBR, GIH, or VBR file included in a folder in the brush search path will show up in the Brushes dialog the next time you start GIMP, or as soon as you press the Refresh button in the Brushes dialog.

> **Note**
> When you create a new parametric brush using the Brush Editor, it is automatically saved in your personal brushes folder.

There are a number of web sites with downloadable collections of GIMP brushes. Rather than supplying a list of links that will soon be out of date, the best advice is to do a search with your favorite search engine for "GIMP brushes". There are also many collections of brushes for other programs with painting functionality. Some can be converted easily into GIMP brushes, some require special conversion utilities, and some cannot be converted at all. Most fancy procedural brush types fall into the last category. If you need to know, look around on the web, and if you don't find anything, look for an expert to ask.

8. The GIH Dialog Box

When your new animated brush is created, it is displayed within the image window and you would like save it into a gih format. You select File → Save as... menu, name your work with the gih extension in the new window relevant field and as soon as you pressed the Save button, the following window is displayed:

Figure 7.18. The dialog to describe the animated brush

This dialog box shows up, if you save an image as GIMP image hose

This dialog box has several options not easy to understand. They allow you to determine the way your brush is animated.

Spacing (Percent)

> "Spacing" is the distance between consecutive brush marks when you trace out a brushstroke with the pointer. You must consider drawing with a brush, whatever the paint tool, like stamping. If Spacing is low, stamps will be very close and stroke look continuous. If spacing is high, stamps will be separated: that's interesting with a color brush (like "green pepper" for instance). Value varies from 1 to 200 and this percentage refers to brush "diameter": 100% is one diameter.

Description

> It's the brush name that will appear at the top of Brush Dialog (grid mode) when the brush is selected.

Cell Size

> That's size of cells you will cut up in layers... Default is one cell per layer and size is that of the layer. Then there is only one brush aspect per layer.

We could have only one big layer and cut up in it the cells that will be used for the different aspects of the animated brush.

For instance, we want a 100x100 pixels brush with 8 different aspects. We can take these 8 aspects from a 400x200 pixels layer, or from a 300x300 pixels layer but with one cell unused.

Number of cells

That's the number of cells (one cell per aspect) that will be cut in every layer. Default is the number of layers as there is only one layer per aspect.

Display as

This tells how cells have been arranged in layers. If, for example, you have placed height cells at the rate of two cells per layer on four layers, GIMP will display: 1 rows of 2 columns on each layer.

Dimension, Ranks, Selection

There things are getting complicated! Explanations are necessary to understand how to arrange cell and layers.

GIMP starts retrieving cells from each layer and stacks them into a FIFO stack (First In First Out: the first in is at the top of the stack and so can be first out). In our example 4 layers with 2 cells in each, we'll have, from top to bottom: first cell of first layer, second cell of first layer, first cell of second layer, second cell of second layer..., second cell of fourth layer. With one cell per layer or with several cells per layer, result is the same. You can see this stack in the Layer Dialog of the resulting .gih image file.

Then GIMP creates a computer array from this stack with the Dimensions you have set. You can use four dimensions.

In computer science an array has a "myarray(x,y,z)" form for a 3 dimensions array (3D). It's easy to imagine a 2D array: on a paper it's an array with rows and columns

With a 3d array we don't talk rows and columns but Dimensions and Ranks. The first dimension is along x axis, the second dimension along y axis, the third along z axis. Each dimension has ranks of cells.

To fill up this array, GIMP starts retrieving cells from the top of stack. The way it fills the array reminds that of an odometer: right rank digits turn first and, when they reach their maximum, left rank digits start running. If you have some memories of Basic programming you will have, with an array(4,2,2), the following succession: (1,1,1),(1,1,2),(1,2,1),(1,2,2),(2,1,1),(2,1,2),(2,2,2),(3,1,1).... (4,2,2). We will see this later in an example.

Besides the rank number that you can give to each dimension, you can also give them a Selection mode. You have several modes that will be applied when drawing:

Incremental

GIMP selects a rank from the concerned dimension according to the order ranks have in that dimension.

Random

GIMP selects a rank at random from the concerned dimension.

Angular

GIMP selects a rank in the concerned dimension according to the moving angle of the brush.

The first rank is for the direction 0°, upwards. The other ranks are affected, clockwise, to an angle whose value is 360/number of ranks. So, with 4 ranks in the concerned dimension, the angle will move 90°

clockwise for each direction change: second rank will be affected to 90° (rightwards), third rank to 180° (downwards) and fourth rank to 270° (-90°) (leftwards).[2]

Speed, Pressure, x tilt, y tilt

These options are for sophisticated drawing tablets.

Examples

A one dimension image pipe

Well! What is all this useful for? We'll see that gradually with examples. You can actually place in each dimension cases that will give your brush a particular action.

Let us start with a 1D brush which will allow us to study selection modes action. We can imagine it like this:

Follow these steps:

1. Open a new 30x30 pixels image, RGB with Transparent fill type. Using the Text tool create 4 layers "1", "2", "3", "4". Delete the "background" layer.
2. Save this image first with .xcf extension to keep its properties then save it as .gih.
3. The Save As Dialog is opened: select a destination for your image. OK. The GIH dialog is opened: Choose Spacing 100, give a name in Description box, 30x30 for Cell Size, 1 dimension, 4 ranks and choose "Incremental" in Selection box. OK.
4. You may have difficulties to save directly in the GIMP Brush directory. In that case, save the .gih file manually into the /usr/share/gimp/gimp/2.0/brushes directory. Then come back into the Toolbox, click in the brush icon to open the Brush Dialog then click on Refresh icon button. Your new brush appears in the Brush window. Select it. Select pencil tool for instance and click and hold with it on a new image:

12341234123412

You see 1, 2, 3, 4 digits following one another in order.

5. Take your .xcf image file back and save it as .gih setting Selection to "Random":

33234241444434

Digits will be displayed at random order.

6. Now select "Angular" Selection:

```
      22222222222
                3
1                3
1                3
 144444444444444
```

A 3 dimensions image hose

We are now going to create a 3D animated brush: its orientation will vary according to brush direction, it will alternate Left/Right hands regularly and its color will vary at random between black and blue.

The first question we have to answer to is the number of images that is necessary. We reserve the first dimension (x) to the brush direction (4 directions). The second dimension (y) is for Left/Right alternation and the third dimension (z) for color variation. Such a brush is represented in a 3D array "myarray(4,2,2)":

There are 4 ranks in first dimension (x), 2 ranks in second dimension (y) and 2 ranks in third dimension (z). We see that there are 4x2x2 = 16 cells. We need 16 images.

1. **Creating images of dimension 1 (x)**

   Open a new 30x30 pixels image, RGB with Transparent Fill Type. Using the zoom draw a left hand with fingers upwards.[3] Save it as handL0k.xcf (hand Left 0° Black).

   Open the Layer Dialog. Double click on the layer to open the Layer Attributes Dialog and rename it to handL0k.

   Duplicate the layer. Let visible only the duplicated layer, select it and apply a 90° rotation (Layer/Transform/ 90° rotation clockwise). Rename it to handL90k.

   Repeat the same operations to create handL180k and handL-90k (or handL270k).

2. **Creating images of dimension 2 (y)**

   This dimension in our example has two ranks, one for left hand and the other for right hand. The left hand rank exists yet. We shall build right hand images by flipping it horizontally.

   Duplicate the handL0k layer. Let it visible only and select it. Rename it to handR0K. Apply Layer/Transform/Flip Horizontally.

   Repeat the same operation on the other left hand layers to create their right hand equivalent.

   Re-order layers to have a clockwise rotation from top to bottom, alternating Left and Right: handL0k, handR0k, handL90k, handR90k, ..., handR-90k.

3. **Creating images of dimension 3 (z)**

   Creating images of dimension 3 (z): The third dimension has two ranks, one for black color and the other for blue color. The first rank, black, exists yet. We well see that images of dimension 3 will be a copy, in blue, of the images of dimension

2. So we will have our 16 images. But a row of 16 layers is not easy to manage: we will use layers with two images.

Select the handL0k layer and let it visible only. Using Image/Canvas Size change canvas size to 60x30 pixels.

Duplicate hand0k layer. On the copy, fill the hand with blue using Bucket Fill tool.

Now, select the Move tool. Double click on it to accede to its properties: check Move the Current Layer option. Move the blue hand into the right part of the layer precisely with the help of Zoom.

Make sure only handL0k and its blue copy are visible. Right click on the Layer Dialog: Apply the Merge Visible Layers command with the option Expand as Necessary. You get a 60x30 pixels layer with the black hand on the left and the blue hand on the right. Rename it to "handsL0".

Repeat the same operations on the other layers.

4. **Set layers in order**

   Layers must be set in order so that GIMP can find the required image at some point of using the brush. Our layers are yet in order but we must understand more generally how to have them in order. There are two ways to imagine this setting in order. The first method is mathematical: GIMP divides the 16 layers first by 4; that gives 4 groups of 4 layers for the first dimension. Each group represents a direction of the brush. Then, it divides each group by 2; that gives 8 groups of 2 layers for the second dimension: each group represents a L/R alternation. Then another division by 2 for the third dimension to represent a color at random between black and blue.

   The other method is visual, by using the array representation. Correlation between two methods is represented in next image:

How will GIMP read this array?: GIMP starts with the first dimension which is programmed for "angular", for instance 90°. In this 90° rank, in yellow, in the second dimension, it selects a L/R alternation, in an "incremental" way. Then, in the third dimension, in a random way, it chooses a color. Finally, our layers must be in the following order:

- handsL0
- handsR0
- handsL90
- handsR90
- handsL180
- handsR180
- handsL270
- handsR270

5. Voilà. Your brush is ready. Save it as .xcf first, then as .gih with the following parameters:
   - Spacing: 100
   - Description: Hands
   - Cell Size: 30x30
   - Number of cells: 16
   - Dimensions: 3
     - Dimension 1: 4 ranks Selection: Angular
     - Dimension 2: 2 ranks Selection: Incremental
     - Dimension 3: 2 ranks Selection: Random

Place your .gih file into GIMP brush directory and refresh the brush box. You can now use your brush.

Figure 7.19. Here is the result by stroking an elliptical selection with the brush:

This brush alternates right hand and left hand regularly, black and blue color at random, direction according to four brush directions.

For previous GIMP versions you may have to replace "clockwise" with "counter-clockwise".

9. Varying brush size

From GIMP-2.4, all brushes have a variable size.

9.1. How to vary the height of a brush

You can get the brush size varying in three ways:

1. Using the Scale slider of the tool that uses the brush. Pencil, Paintbrush, Eraser, Airbrush, Clone, Heal, Perspective Clone, Blur/Sharpen and Dodge/Burn tools have a slider to vary brush size.

   Figure 7.20. The Scale slider

2. By programming the mouse wheel:
     1. In the main window of GIMP, click on Edit → Preferences.
     2. In the left column of the new window, select Input Devices → Input Controllers.

3. You can see Additional Input Controllers, with two columns: Available Controllers and Active Controllers.

   In the column Active Controllers, double-click the Main Mouse Wheel button.

4. Then, you see a new window: Configure Input Controller.

   In the left column Event, click Scroll Up to get it highlighted.

5. Click the Edit button (at the bottom middle of the list).
6. You can see the window Select Controller Event Action.

   Drop-down the Tools item, by clicking the small triangle on its left.

7. In the left column Action, click Increase Brush Scale to highlight it, then click the OK button.
8. Now, in front of Scroll Up is display tools-paint-brush-scale-increase.
9. Close the window.
10. With the same method, program Scroll Down with Decrease Brush Scale.
11. Don't forget to click the OK button of the main window of Preferences.

After these somewhat long explanations, you can use your mouse wheel to vary size brush. For example, choose the pencil tool with the "Circle" brush. Set the pointer in the image window, use the mouse wheel, in the two directions, you can see the "Circle" shrinking or stretching.

3. You can program the "Up" and "Down" arrow keys of the keyboard.

   The method is similar to that of the mouse wheel. The only differences are:

   - In the column Active Controllers, double-click Main Keyboard.
   - In the column Event, click Cursor Up for the first key, and Cursor Down for the second key.
   - Then, use the two keys (Up arrow and Down arrow) and the result is the same as you got with the mouse wheel.

9.2. Creating a brush quickly

Two methods to create a new brush easily:

1. First, the "superfast" method. You have an image area you want make a brush from it, to be used with a tool like pencil, airbrush... Select it with the rectangular (or elliptical) select tool, then do a Copy of this selection and immediately you can see this copy in the first position of the Brush Dialog, and its name is "Clipboard". It is immediately usable.

    Figure 7.21. Selection becomes a brush after copying

2. The second method is more elaborate.

    Do File → New with, for example, a width and a length of 35 pixels and in the advanced options a Color Space in Gray Level and Fill with: white.

    Zoom on this new image to enlarge it and draw on it with a black pencil.

    Save it with a .gbr extension in the directory /home/name_of_user/.gimp-2.8/brushes/.

    In the Brushes dialog window, click on the button Refresh brushes 🔄 And your marvellous brush appears right in the middle of the other brushes. You can use it immediately, without starting GIMP again.

Figure 7.22. Steps to create a brush

Draw image, save as brush

Refresh brushes

Use the brush

10. Gradients

Figure 7.23. Some examples of GIMP gradients.

Gradients from top to bottom: FG to BG (RGB); Full saturation spectrum; Nauseating headache; Browns; Four bars

A *gradient* is a set of colors arranged in a linear order. The most basic use of gradients is by the **Blend tool**, sometimes known as the "gradient tool" or "gradient fill tool": it works by filling the selection with colors from a gradient. You have many options to choose from for controlling the way the gradient colors are arranged within the selection. There are also other important ways to use gradients, including:

Painting with a gradient

> Each of GIMP's basic painting tools allows you the option of using colors from a gradient. This enables you to create brushstrokes that change color from one end to the other.

The Gradient Map filter

> This filter is now in the Colors menu, and allows you to "colorize" an image, using the color intensity of each point with the corresponding color from the active gradient (the intensity 0, very dark, is replaced by the color at most left end of the gradient, progressively until the intensity is 255, very light, replaced by the most right color of the gradient. See **Section 8.23, "Gradient Map"** for more information.

When you install GIMP, it comes presupplied with a large number of interesting gradients, and you can add new ones that you create or download from other sources. You can access the full set of available gradients using the **Gradients dialog,** a dockable dialog that you can either activate when you need it, or keep around as a tab in a dock. The "current gradient", used in most gradient-related operations, is shown in the Brush/Pattern/Gradient area of the Toolbox. Clicking on the gradient symbol in the Toolbox is an alternative way of bringing up the Gradients dialog.

Many quickly examples of working with gradient (for more information see **Blend Tool):**

- Put a gradient in a selection:
  1. Choose a gradient.
  2. With the Blend Tool click and drag with the mouse between two points of a selection.
  3. Colors will distributed perpendicularly to the direction of the drag of the mouse and according to the length of it.

Figure 7.24. How to use rapidly a gradient in a selection

- Painting with a gradient:

    You can also use a gradient with the Pencil, Paintbrush or Airbrush tools if you choose the dynamics Color From Gradient. In the next step choose a suitable gradient from Color options and in the Fade options set the gradients length and the style of the repeating. The chapter **Section 3.2.6, "Dynamics Options"** describes these parameters in more detail.

    The following example shows the impact on the Pencil tool. You see in the upper side of the figure the necessary settings and the lower side of the figure shows the resulting succession of the gradients colors.

    Figure 7.25. How to use rapidly a gradient with a drawing tool

    To use the Paint tools with the same settings as they were known as option Use color from gradient in GIMP up to version 2.6 open the **Tool Presets Dialog**. Then choose one of the items Airbrush (Color

From Gradient), Paintbrush (Color From Gradient) or Pencil (Color From Gradient) from it.

- Different productions with the same gradient:

Figure 7.26. Gradient usage

Four ways of using the Tropical Colors gradient: a linear gradient fill, a shaped gradient fill, a stroke painted using colors from a gradient, and a stroke painted with a fuzzy brush then colored using the Gradient Map filter.

A few useful things to know about GIMP's gradients:

- The first four gradients in the list are special: they use the Foreground and Background colors from the Toolbox Color Area, instead of being fixed. FG to BG (RGB) is the RGB representation of the gradient from the Foreground color to the Background color in Toolbox. FG to BG (HSV counter-clockwise) represents the hue succession in Color Circle from the selected hue to 360°. FG to BG (HSV clockwise represents the hue succession in Color Circle from the selected hue to 0°. With FG to transparent , the selected hue becomes more and more transparent. You can modify these colors by using the Color Selector. Thus, by altering the foreground and background colors, you can make these gradients transition smoothly between any two colors you want.
- Gradients can involve not just color changes, but also changes in opacity. Some of the gradients are completely opaque; others include transparent or translucent parts. When you fill or paint with a non-opaque gradient, the existing contents of the layer will show through behind it.
- You can create new *custom* gradients, using the Gradient Editor. You cannot modify the gradients that are supplied with GIMP, but you can duplicate them or create new ones, and then edit those.

The gradients that are supplied with GIMP are stored in a system gradients folder. By default, gradients that you create are stored in a folder called gradients in your personal GIMP directory. Any gradient files (ending with the extension .ggr) found in one of these folders, will automatically be loaded when you start GIMP. You can add more directories to the gradient search path, if you want to, in the Gradients tab of the **Data Folders** pages of the Preferences dialog.

New in GIMP 2.2 is the ability to load gradient files in SVG format, used by many vector graphics programs. To make GIMP load an SVG gradient file, all you need to do is place it in the gradients folder of your personal GIMP directory, or any other folder in your gradient search path.

Tip

You can find a large number of interesting SVG gradients on the web, in particular at OpenClipArt Gradients OPENCLIPART-GRADIENT. You won't be able to see what these gradients look like unless your browser supports SVG, but that won't prevent you from downloading them.

11. Patterns

A *pattern* is an image, usually small, used for filling regions by *tiling*, that is, by placing copies of the pattern side by side like ceramic tiles. A pattern is said to be *tileable* if copies of it can be adjoined left-edge-to-right-edge and top-edge-to-bottom-edge without creating obvious seams. Not all useful patterns are tileable, but tileable patterns are nicest for many purposes. (A *texture*, by the way, is the same thing as a pattern.)

Figure 7.27. Pattern usage

Three ways of using the "Leopard" pattern: bucket-filling a selection, painting with the Clone tool, and stroking an elliptical selection with the pattern.

In GIMP there are three main uses for patterns:

- With the Bucket Fill tool, you can choose to fill a region with a pattern instead of a solid color.

    Figure 7.28. The checked box for use a pattern

    The box for pattern fill is checked and a click on the pattern shows you all patterns in grid mode.

- With the Clone tool, you can paint using a pattern, with a wide variety of paintbrush shapes.
- When you *stroke* a path or selection, you can do it with a pattern instead of a solid color. You can also use the Clone tool as your choice if you stroke the selection using a painting tool.

Tip

Note: Patterns do not need to be opaque. If you fill or paint using a pattern with translucent or transparent areas, then the previous contents of the area will show through from behind it. This is one of many ways of doing "overlays" in GIMP.

When you install GIMP, it comes presupplied with a few dozen patterns, which seem to have been chosen more or less randomly. You can also add new patterns, either ones you create yourself, or ones you download from the vast number available online.

GIMP's *current pattern*, used in most pattern-related operations, is shown in the Brush/Pattern/Gradient area of the Toolbox. Clicking on the pattern symbol brings up the **Patterns dialog**, which allows you to select a different pattern. You can also access the Patterns dialog by menu, or dock it so that it is present continuously.

To add a new pattern to the collection, so that it shows up in the Patterns dialog, you need to save it in a format GIMP can use, in a folder included in GIMP's pattern search path. There are several file formats you can use for patterns:

PAT

> The .pat format is used for patterns which were created specifically for GIMP. You can convert any image into a .pat file by opening it in GIMP and then saving it using a file name ending in .pat.
>
> **Caution**
>
> Do not confuse GIMP-generated .pat files with files created by other programs (e.g. Photoshop) – after all, .pat is just a part of an (arbitrary) file name.
>
> (However, GIMP *does* support Photoshop .pat files until a certain version.)

PNG, JPEG, BMP, GIF, TIFF

> Since GIMP 2.2 you can use .png, .jpg, .bmp, .gif, or .tiff files as patterns.

To make a pattern available, you place it in one of the folders in GIMP's pattern search path. By default, the pattern search path includes two folders, the system patterns folder, which you should not use or alter, and the patterns folder inside your personal GIMP directory. You can add new folders to the pattern search path using the **Pattern Folders** page of the Preferences dialog. Any PAT file (or, in GIMP 2.2, any of the other acceptable formats) included in a folder in the pattern search path will show up in the Patterns dialog the next time you start GIMP.

There are countless ways of creating interesting patterns in GIMP, using the wide variety of available tools and filters -- particularly the rendering filters. You can find tutorials for this in many locations, including the GIMP home page [GIMP]. Some of the filters have options that allows you to make their results tileable. Also, see **Section 2.7, "Tileable Blur**", this filter allows you to blend the edges of an image in order to make it more smoothly tileable.

Figure 7.29. Pattern script examples

Examples of patterns created using six of the Pattern Script-Fu's that come with GIMP. Default settings were used for everything except size. (From left to right: 3D Truchet; Camouflage; Flatland; Land; Render Map; Swirly)

Also of interest are a set of pattern-generating scripts that come with GIMP: you can find them in the menu bar, through File → Create → Patterns. Each of the scripts creates a new image filled with a particular type of pattern: a dialog pops up that allows you to set parameters controlling the details of the appearance. Some of these patterns are most useful for cutting and pasting; others serve best as bumpmaps.

Figure 7.30. How to create new patterns

12. Palettes

A *palette* is a set of discrete colors. In GIMP, palettes are used mainly for two purposes:

- They allow you to paint with a selected set of colors, in the same way an oil painter works with colors from a limited number of tubes.
- They form the colormaps of indexed images. An indexed image can use a maximum of 256 different colors, but these can be any colors. The colormap of an indexed image is called an "indexed palette" in GIMP.

Actually neither of these functions fall very much into the mainstream of GIMP usage: it is possible to do rather sophisticated things in GIMP without ever dealing with palettes. Still, they are something that an advanced user should understand, and even a less advanced user may need to think about them in some situations, as for example when working with GIF files.

Figure 7.31. The Palettes dialog

When you install GIMP, it comes supplied with several dozen predefined palettes, and you can also create new ones. Some of the predefined palettes are commonly useful, such as the "Web" palette, which contains the set of colors considered "web safe"; many of the palettes seem to have been chosen more or less whimsically. You can access all of the available palettes using the **Palettes dialog**. This is also the starting point if you want to create a new palette.

Figure 7.32. The Palette Editor

Double-clicking on a palette in the Palettes dialog brings up the Palette Editor, showing the colors from the palette you clicked on. You can use this to paint with the palette: clicking on a color sets GIMP's foreground to that color, as shown in the Color Area of the Toolbox. Holding down the **Ctrl** key while clicking, on the other hand, sets GIMP's background color to the color you click on.

You can also, as the name implies, use the Palette Editor to change the colors in a palette, so long as it is a palette that you have created yourself. You cannot edit the palettes that are supplied with GIMP; however you can duplicate them and then edit the copies.

When you create palettes using the Palette Editor, they are automatically saved as soon as you exit GIMP, in the palettes folder of your personal GIMP directory. Any palette files in this directory, or in the system palettes directory created when GIMP is installed, are automatically loaded and shown in the Palettes dialog the next time you start GIMP. You can also add other folders to the palette search path using the Palette Folders page of the Preferences dialog.

GIMP palettes are stored using a special file format, in files with the extension .gpl. It is a very simple format, and they are ASCII files, so if you happen to obtain palettes from another source, and would like to use them in GIMP, it probably won't be very hard to convert them: just take a look at any .gpl and you will see what to do.

12.1. Colormap

Confusingly, GIMP makes use of two types of palettes. The more noticeable are the type shown in the Palettes dialog: palettes that exist independently of any image. The second type, *indexed palettes*, form the colormaps of indexed images. Each indexed image has its own private indexed palette, defining the set of colors available in the image: the maximum number of colors allowed in an indexed palette is 256. These palettes are called "indexed" because each color is associated with an index number. (Actually, the colors in ordinary palettes are numbered as well, but the numbers have no functional significance.)

Figure 7.33. The Colormap dialog

The colormap of an indexed image is shown in the **Indexed Palette dialog**, which should not be confused with the Palettes dialog. The Palettes dialog shows a list of all of the palettes available; the Colormap dialog shows the colormap of the currently active image, if it is an indexed image – otherwise it shows nothing.

You can, however, create an ordinary palette from the colors in an indexed image—actually from the colors in any image. To do this, choose Import Palette from the right-click popup menu in the Palettes dialog: this pops up a dialog that gives you several options, including the option to import the palette from an image. (You can also import any of GIMP's gradients as a palette.) This possibility becomes important if you want to create a set of indexed images that all use the same set of colors.

When you convert an image into indexed mode, a major part of the process is the creation of an indexed palette for the image. How this happens is described in detail in **Section 6.6, "Indexed mode"**. Briefly, you have several methods to choose from, one of which is to use a specified palette from the Palettes dialog.

Thus, to sum up the foregoing, ordinary palettes can be turned into indexed palettes when you convert an image into indexed mode; indexed palettes can be turned into ordinary palettes by importing them into the Palettes dialog.

Figure 7.34. Colormap dialog (1) and Palette dialog (2)

13. Presets

If you often use tools with particular settings, presets are for you. You can save these settings and get them back when you want.

Paint tools, which are normally in Toolbox, have a preset system that have been much improved with GIMP-2.8. Color tools (except Posterize and Desaturate), which are not normally in Toolbox, have their own preset system.

Four buttons at the bottom of all tools options dialogs allow you to save, restore, delete or reset presets.

Paint tool presets are described in **Section 5.1, "Tool Presets Dialog"**.

Color tool presets are described in **Section 5.1.1, "Color Tool Presets"**.

14. Drawing Simple Objects

In this section, you will learn how to create simple objects in GIMP. It's pretty easy once you figure out how to do it. GIMP provides a huge set of **Tools** and Shortcuts which most new users get lost in.

14.1. Drawing a Straight Line

Let's begin by painting a straight line. The easiest way to create a straight line is by using your favorite **brush tool,** the mouse and the keyboard.

Procedure 7.1. Drawing a Straight Line

1. **Figure 7.35. A new image**

    The dialog shows a new image, filled with a white background.

    Create a new image. Select your favorite brush tool or use the pencil, if in doubt. Select a foreground color, but be sure that the foreground and background colors are different.

2. **Figure 7.36. The start of the straight line**

The dialog shows a new image, with the first dot which indicates the start of the straight line. The dot has a black foreground color.

Create a starting point by clicking on the image display area with the left mouse button. Your canvas should look similar to **Figure 7.35, "A new image"**.

3. **Figure 7.37. The helpline**

The screenshot shows the helpline, which indicates how the finished line will look.

Now, hold down the **Shift** button on your keyboard and move the mouse away from the starting point you created. You'll see a thin line indicating how the line will look.

4. **Figure 7.38. The line after the second click**

The line created appears in the image window after drawing the second point (or end point), while the **Shift** key is still pressed.

If you're satisfied with the direction and length of the line, click the left mouse button again to finish the line. The GIMP displays a straight line now. If the line doesn't appear, check the foreground and background colors and be sure that you kept the **Shift** key pressed while painting. You can keep creating lines by continuing to hold the **Shift** key and creating additional end points.

14. Drawing Simple Objects

In this section, you will learn how to create simple objects in GIMP. It's pretty easy once you figure out how to do it. GIMP provides a huge set of Tools and Shortcuts which most new users get lost in.

14.1. Drawing a Straight Line

Let's begin by painting a straight line. The easiest way to create a straight line is by using your favorite brush tool, the mouse and the keyboard.

Procedure 7.1. Drawing a Straight Line

1. **Figure 7.35. A new image**

   The dialog shows a new image, filled with a white background.

   Create a new image. Select your favorite brush tool or use the pencil, if in doubt. Select a foreground color, but be sure that the foreground and background colors are different.

2. **Figure 7.36. The start of the straight line**

   The dialog shows a new image, with the first dot which indicates the start of the straight line. The dot has a black foreground color.

   Create a starting point by clicking on the image display area with the left mouse button. Your canvas should look similar to **Figure 7.35, "A new image"**.

3. **Figure 7.37. The helpline**

   The screenshot shows the helpline, which indicates how the finished line will look.

   Now, hold down the **Shift** button on your keyboard and move the mouse away from the starting point you created. You'll see a thin line indicating how the line will look.

4. **Figure 7.38. The line after the second click**

   The line created appears in the image window after drawing the second point (or end point), while the **Shift** key is still pressed.

   If you're satisfied with the direction and length of the line, click the left mouse button again to finish the line. The GIMP displays a straight line now. If the line doesn't appear, check the foreground and background colors and be sure that you kept the **Shift** key pressed while painting. You can keep creating lines by continuing to hold the **Shift** key and creating additional end points.

14.2. Creating a Basic Shape

1. GIMP is not designed to be used for drawing.[4] However, you may create shapes by either painting them using the technique described in **Section 14.1, "Drawing a Straight Line"** or by using the selection tools. Of course, there are various other ways to paint a shape, but we'll stick to the easiest ones here. So, create a new image and check that the foreground and background colors are different.
2. **Figure 7.39. Creating a rectangular selection**

The screenshot shows how a rectangular selection is created. Press and hold the left mouse button while you move the mouse in the direction of the red arrow.

Basic shapes like rectangles or ellipses, can be created using the selection tools. This tutorial uses a rectangular selection as an example. So, choose the rectangular selection tool and create a new selection: press and hold the left mouse button while you move the mouse to another position in the image (illustrated in figure **Figure 7.39, "Creating a rectangular selection"**). The selection is created when you release the mouse button. For more information about key modifiers see **selection tools.**

3. **Figure 7.40. Rectangular selection filled with foreground color**

The screenshot shows a rectangular selection filled with the foreground color.

After creating the selection, you can either create a filled or an outlined shape with the foreground color of your choice. If you go for the first option, choose a foreground color and fill the selection with the bucket fill tool. If you choose the latter option, create an outline by using theStroke selection menu item from the Edit menu. If you're satisfied with the result, remove the selection.

Chapter 8. Combining Images

1. Introduction to Layers

A good way to visualize a GIMP image is as a stack of transparencies: in GIMP terminology, each individual transparency is called a *layer*. There is no limit, in principle, to the number of layers an image can have: only the amount of memory available on the system. It is not uncommon for advanced users to work with images containing dozens of layers.

The organization of layers in an image is shown by the Layers dialog, which is the second most important type of dialog window in GIMP, after the Main Toolbox. The appearance of the Layers dialog is shown in the adjoining illustration. How it works is described in detail in the Layers Dialog section, but we will touch on some aspects of it here, in relation to the layer properties that they display.

Each open image has at any time a single *active drawable*. A "drawable" is a GIMP concept that includes layers, but also several other types of things, such as channels, layer masks, and the selection mask. (Basically, a "drawable" is anything that can be drawn on with painting tools). If a layer is currently active, it is shown highlighted in the Layers dialog, and its name is shown in the status area of the image window. If not, you can activate it by clicking on it. If none of the layers are highlighted, it means the active drawable is something other than a layer.

In the menubar above an image window, you can find a menu called Layer, containing a number of commands that affect the active layer of the image. The same menu can be accessed by right-clicking in the Layers dialog.

1.1. Layer Properties

Each layer in an image has a number of important attributes:

Name

> Every layer has a name. This is assigned automatically when the layer is created, but you can change it. You can change the name of a layer either by double-clicking on it in the Layers dialog, or by right-clicking there and then selecting the top entry in the menu that appears, Edit Layer Attributes.

Presence or absence of an alpha channel

An alpha channel encodes information about how transparent a layer is at each pixel. It is visible in the Channel Dialog: white is complete opacity, black is complete transparency and grey levels are partial transparencies.

The background layer is particular. If you have just created a new image, it has still only one layer which is a background layer. If the image has been created with an opaque Fill type, this one layer has no Alpha channel. If you add a new layer, even with an opaque Fill type, an Alpha channel is automatically created, which applies to all layers apart from the background layer. To get a background layer with transparency, either you create your new image with a transparent Fill type, or you use the Add an Alpha Channel.

Every layer other than the bottom layer of an image has automatically an Alpha channel, but you can't see a grayscale representation of the alpha values. See **Alpha** in Glossary for more information.

Example for Alpha channel.

Figure 8.1. Alpha channel example: Basic image

This image has three layers painted with pure 100% opaque Red, Green, and Blue. In the Channel Dialog, you can see that an alpha Channel has been added. It is white because the image is not transparent since there is at least one 100% opaque layer. The current layer is the red one : since it is painted with pure red, there is no green and no blue and the corresponding channels are black.

Figure 8.2. Alpha channel example: One transparent layer

The left part of the first layer has been made transparent (Rectangular selection, Edit/Clear). The second layer, green, is visible. The Alpha channel is still white, since there is an opaque layer in this part of the image.

Figure 8.3. Alpha channel example: Two transparent layers

The left part of the second layer has been made transparent. The third layer, blue, is visible through the first and second layers. The Alpha channel is still white, since there is an opaque layer in this part of the image.

Figure 8.4. Alpha channel example: Three transparent layers

The left part of the third layer has been made transparent. The Alpha channel is still white and the left part of the layer is white, opaque! The background layer has no Alpha channel. In this case, the Clear command works like the Eraser and uses the Background color of Toolbox.

Figure 8.5. Alpha channel example: Alpha channel added to the Background

We used the Layer → Transparency → Add Alpha Channel command, on the Background layer. Now, the left part of the image is fully transparent and has the color of the page the image is lying on. The left part of the Alpha Channel thumbnail is black (transparent) in the Channel Dialog.

Layer type

The layer type is determined by the image type (see previous section) and the presence or absence of an alpha channel. These are the possible layer types:

- RGB
- RGBA
- Gray
- GrayA
- Indexed
- IndexedA

The main reason this matters is that most filters (in the Filters menu) only accept a subset of layer types, and appear grayed out in the menu if the active layer does not have an acceptable type. Often you can rectify this either by changing the mode of the image or by adding or removing an alpha channel.

👁 Visibility

> It is possible to remove a layer from an image, without destroying it, by clicking on the symbol in the Layers dialog. This is called "toggling the visibility" of the layer. Most operations on an image treat toggled-off layers as if they did not exist. When you work with images containing many layers, with varying opacity, you often can get a better picture of the contents of the layer you want to work on by hiding some of the other layers.
>
> **ⓘ Tip**
>
> If you *Shift*-click on the eye symbol, this will cause all layers *except* the one you click on to be hidden.

Linkage to other layers

> If you click between the eye icon and the layer thumbnail, you get a chain icon, which enables you to group layers for operations on multiple layers (for example with the Move tool or a transform tool).
>
> **Figure 8.6. Layer Dialog**
>
> Red: Linkage to others layers. Green: Visibility.

Size and boundaries

> In GIMP, the boundaries of a layer do not necessarily match the boundaries of the image that contains it. When you create text, for example, each text item goes into its own separate layer, and the layer is precisely sized to contain the text and nothing more. Also, when you create a new layer using cut-and-paste, the new layer is sized just large enough to contain the pasted item. In the image window, the boundaries of the currently active layer are shown outlined with a black-and-yellow dashed line.
>
> The main reason why this matters is that you cannot do anything to a layer outside of its boundaries: you can't act on what doesn't exist. If this causes you problems, you can alter the dimensions of the layer

using any of several commands that you can find near the bottom of the Layer menu.

> **Note**
>
> The amount of memory that a layer consumes is determined by its dimensions, not its contents. So, if you are working with large images or images that contain many layers, it might pay off to trim layers to the minimum possible size.

Opacity

The opacity of a layer determines the extent to which it lets colors from layers beneath it in the stack show through. Opacity ranges from 0 to 100, with 0 meaning complete transparency, and 100 meaning complete opacity.

Mode

The Mode of a layer determines how colors from the layer are combined with colors from the underlying layers to produce a visible result. This is a sufficiently complex, and sufficiently important, concept to deserve a section of its own, which follows. See **Section 2, "Layer Modes"**.

Layer mask

In addition to the alpha channel, there is another way to control the transparency of a layer: by adding a *layer mask*, which is an extra grayscale drawable associated with the layer. A layer does not have a layer mask by default: it must be added specifically. Layer masks, and how to work with them, are described much more extensively in the Layer Mask section.

"Lock alpha channel" setting

In the upper left corner of the Layers dialog appears a small checkbox that controls the "Lock" setting for the transparency of the layer (see the figure below). If this is checked, then the alpha channel for the layer is locked, and no manipulation has any effect on it. In particular, nothing that you do to a transparent part of the layer will have any effect.

Figure 8.7. Lock Alpha channel

2. Layer Modes

GIMP has twenty-one layer modes. Layer modes are also sometimes called "blending modes". Selecting a layer mode changes the appearance of the layer or image, based on the layer or layers beneath it. If there is only one layer, the layer mode has no effect. There must therefore be at least two layers in the image to be able to use layer modes.

You can set the layer mode in the Mode menu in the Layers dialog. GIMP uses the layer mode to determine how to combine each pixel in the top layer with the pixel in the same location in the layer below it.

> **Note**
>
> There is a drop-down list in the Toolbox options box which contains modes that affect the painting tools in a similar way to the layer modes. You can use all of the same modes for painting that are available for layers, and there are two additional modes just for the painting tools. See **Section 3.3, "Brush Tools (Pencil, Paintbrush, Airbrush)"**.

Layer modes permit complex color changes in the image. They are often used with a new layer which acts as a kind of mask. For example, if you put a solid white layer over an image and set the layer mode of the new layer to "Saturation", the underlying visible layers will appear in shades of gray.

Figure 8.8. Images (masks) for layer mode examples

Mask 1   Mask 2

Figure 8.9. Images (backgrounds) for layer mode examples

Key fob   Ducks

In the descriptions of the layer modes below, the equations are also shown. This is for those who are curious about the mathematics of the layer modes. You do not need to understand the equations in order to use the layer modes effectively, however.

The equations are in a shorthand notation. For example, the equation

Equation 8.1. Example

$$E = M + I$$

means, " For each pixel in the upper (*M*ask)and lower (*I*mage) layer, add each of the corresponding color components together to form the *E* resulting pixel's color. " Pixel color components must always be between 0 and 255.

> **Note**
>
> Unless the description below says otherwise, a negative color component is set to 0 and a color component larger than 255 is set to 255.

The examples below show the effects of each of the modes.

Since the results of each mode vary greatly depending upon the colors on the layers, these images can only give you a general idea of how the modes work. You are encouraged to try them out yourself. You might start with two similar layers, where one is a copy of the other, but slightly modified (by being blurred, moved, rotated, scaled, color-inverted, etc.) and seeing what happens with the layer modes.

Normal

Figure 8.10. Example for layer mode "Normal"

Both images are blended into each other with the same intensity.

With 100% opacity only the upper layer is shown when blending with "Normal".

Normal mode is the default layer mode. The layer on top covers the layers below it. If you want to see anything below the top layer when you use this mode, the layer must have some transparent areas.

The equation is:

Equation 8.2. Equation for layer mode "Normal"

Dissolve

Figure 8.11. Example for layer mode "Dissolve"

Both images are blended into each other with the same intensity.

With 100% opacity only the upper layer is shown when blending wit

Dissolve mode dissolves the upper layer into the layer beneath it by drawing a random pattern of pixels in areas of partial transparency. It is useful as a layer mode, but it is also often useful as a painting mode.

This is especially visible along the edges within an image. It is easiest to see in an enlarged screenshot. The image on the left illustrates "Normal" layer mode (enlarged) and the image on the right shows the same two layers in "Dissolve" mode, where it can be clearly seen how the pixels are dispersed.

Figure 8.12. Enlarged screenshots

Normal mode.   Dissolve mode.

Multiply

Figure 8.13. Example for layer mode "Multiply"

Mask 1 is used as upper layer with 100% opacity.

Mask 2 is used as upper layer with 100% opacity.

Multiply mode multiplies the pixel values of the upper layer with those of the layer below it and then divides the result by 255. The result is usually a darker image. If either layer is white, the resulting image is the same as the other layer (1 * I = I). If either layer is black, the resulting image is completely black (0 * I = 0).

The equation is:

Equation 8.3. Equation for layer mode "Multiply"

The mode is commutative; the order of the two layers doesn't matter.

Divide

Figure 8.14. Example for layer mode "Divide"

Mask 1 is used as upper layer with 100% opacity. Mask 2 is used as upper layer with 100% opacity.

Divide mode multiplies each pixel value in the lower layer by 256 and then divides that by the corresponding pixel value of the upper layer plus one. (Adding one to the denominator avoids dividing by zero.) The resulting image is often lighter, and sometimes looks "burned out".

The equation is:

Equation 8.4. Equation for layer mode "Divide"

$$E = \frac{256 \times I}{M + 1}$$

Screen

Figure 8.15. Example for layer mode "Screen"

Mask 1 is used as upper layer with 100% opacity.

Mask 2 is used as upper layer with 100% opacity.

Screen mode inverts the values of each of the visible pixels in the two layers of the image. (That is, it subtracts each of them from 255.) Then it multiplies them together, divides by 255 and inverts this value again. The resulting image is usually brighter, and sometimes "washed out" in appearance. The exceptions to this are a black layer, which does not change the other layer, and a white layer, which results in a white image. Darker colors in the image appear to be more transparent.

The equation is:

Equation 8.5. Equation for layer mode "Screen"

$$E = 255 - \frac{(255 - M) \times (255 - I)}{255}$$

The mode is commutative; the order of the two layers doesn't matter.

Overlay

Figure 8.16. Example for layer mode "Overlay"

Mask 1 is used as upper layer with 100% opacity.

Mask 2 is used as upper layer with 100% opacity.

Overlay mode inverts the pixel value of the lower layer, multiplies it by two times the pixel value of the upper layer, adds that to the original pixel value of the lower layer, divides by 255, and then multiplies by the pixel value of the original lower layer and divides by 255 again. It darkens the image, but not as much as with "Multiply" mode.

The equation is: [5]

Equation 8.6. Equation for layer mode "Overlay"

$$E = \frac{I}{255} \times \left(I + \frac{2 \times M}{255} \times (255 - I) \right)$$

Dodge

Figure 8.17. Example for layer mode "Dodge"

Mask 1 is used as upper layer with 100% opacity.

Mask 2 is used as upper layer with 100% opacity.

Dodge mode multiplies the pixel value of the lower layer by 256, then divides that by the inverse of the pixel value of the top layer. The resulting image is usually lighter, but some colors may be inverted.

In photography, dodging is a technique used in a darkroom to decrease the exposure in particular areas of the image. This brings out details in the shadows. When used for this purpose, dodge may work best on Grayscale images and with a painting tool, rather than as a layer mode.

The equation is:

Equation 8.7. Equation for layer mode "Dodge"

$$E = \frac{256 \times I}{(255 - M) + 1}$$

Burn

Figure 8.18. Example for layer mode "Burn"

Mask 1 is used as upper layer with 100% opacity.

Mask 2 is used as upper layer with 100% opacity.

Burn mode inverts the pixel value of the lower layer, multiplies it by 256, divides that by one plus the pixel value of the upper layer, then inverts the result. It tends to make the image darker, somewhat similar to "Multiply" mode.

In photography, burning is a technique used in a darkroom to increase the exposure in particular areas of the image. This brings out details in the highlights. When used for this purpose, burn may work best on Grayscale images and with a painting tool, rather than as a layer mode.

The equation is:

Equation 8.8. Equation for layer mode "Burn"

$$E = 255 - \frac{256 \times (255 - I)}{M + 1}$$

Hard light

Figure 8.19. Example for layer mode "Hard light"

Mask 1 is used as upper layer with 100% opacity.

Mask 2 is used as upper layer with 100% opacity.

Hard light mode is rather complicated because the equation consists of two parts, one for darker colors and one for brighter colors. If the pixel color of the upper layer is greater than 128, the layers are combined according to the first formula shown below. Otherwise, the pixel values of the upper and lower layers are multiplied together and multiplied by two, then divided by 256. You might use this mode to combine two photographs and obtain bright colors and sharp edges.

The equation is complex and different according to the value >128 or ≤ 128:

Equation 8.9. Equation for layer mode "Hard light", M > 128

$$E = 255 - \frac{(255 - 2 \times (M - 128)) \times (255 - I)}{256}, \quad M > 128$$

Equation 8.10. Equation for layer mode "Hard light", M ≤ 128

$$E = \frac{2 \times M \times I}{256}, \quad M \leq 128$$

Soft light

Figure 8.20. Example for layer mode "Soft light"

Mask 1 is used as upper layer with 100% opacity.

Mask 2 is used as upper layer with 100% opacity.

Soft light is not related to "Hard light" in anything but the name, but it does tend to make the edges softer and the colors not so bright. It is similar to "Overlay" mode. In some versions of GIMP, "Overlay" mode and "Soft light" mode are identical.

The equation is complicated. It needs Rs, the result of Screen mode :

Equation 8.11. Equation for layer mode "Screen"

$$R_s = 255 - \frac{(255 - M) \times (255 - I)}{255}$$

Equation 8.12. Equation for layer mode "Soft light"

$$E = \frac{(255 - I) \times M + R_s}{255} \times I$$

Grain extract

Figure 8.21. Example for layer mode "Grain extract"

Mask 1 is used as upper layer with 100% opacity.

Mask 2 is used as upper layer with 100% opacity.

Grain extract mode is supposed to extract the "film grain" from a layer to produce a new layer that is pure grain, but it can also be useful for giving images an embossed appearance. It subtracts the pixel value of the upper layer from that of the lower layer and adds 128.

The equation is:

Equation 8.13. Equation for layer mode "Grain extract"

$$E = I - M + 128$$

Grain merge

There are two more layer modes, but these are available only for painting tools. See Painting Modes for detailed information.

Figure 8.22. Example for layer mode "Grain merge"

Mask 1 is used as upper layer with 100% opacity.

Mask 2 is used as upper layer with 100% opacity.

Grain merge mode merges a grain layer (possibly one created from the "Grain extract" mode) into the current layer, leaving a grainy version of the original layer. It does just the opposite of "Grain extract". It adds the pixel values of the upper and lower layers together and subtracts 128.

The equation is:

Equation 8.14. Equation for layer mode "Grain merge"

$$E = I + M - 128$$

Difference

Figure 8.23. Example for layer mode "Difference"

Mask 1 is used as upper layer with 100% opacity.

Mask 2 is used as upper layer with 100% opacity.

Difference mode subtracts the pixel value of the upper layer from that of the lower layer and then takes the absolute value of the result. No matter what the original two layers look like, the result looks rather odd. You can use it to invert elements of an image.

The equation is:

Equation 8.15. Equation for layer mode "Difference"

$$E = |I - M|$$

The mode is commutative; the order of the two layers doesn't matter.

Addition

Figure 8.24. Example for layer mode "Addition"

Mask 1 is used as upper layer with 100% opacity.

Mask 2 is used as upper layer with 100% opacity.

Addition mode is very simple. The pixel values of the upper and lower layers are added to each other. The resulting image is usually lighter. The equation can result in color values greater than 255, so some of the light colors may be set to the maximum value of 255.

The equation is:

Equation 8.16. Equation for layer mode "Addition"

$$E = \min((M + I), 255)$$

The mode is commutative; the order of the two layers doesn't matter.

Subtract

Figure 8.25. Example for layer mode "Subtract"

Mask 1 is used as upper layer with 100% opacity.

Mask 2 is used as upper layer with 100% opacity.

Subtract mode subtracts the pixel values of the upper layer from the pixel values of the lower layer. The resulting image is normally darker. You might get a lot of black or near-black in the resulting image. The equation can result in negative color values, so some of the dark colors may be set to the minimum value of 0.

The equation is:

Equation 8.17. Equation for layer mode "Subtraction"

$$E = \max((I - M), 0)$$

Darken only

Figure 8.26. Example for layer mode "Darken only"

Mask 1 is used as upper layer with 100% opacity.

Mask 2 is used as upper layer with 100% opacity.

Darken only mode compares each component of each pixel in the upper layer with the corresponding one in the lower layer and uses the smaller value in the resulting image. Completely white layers have no effect on the final image and completely black layers result in a black image.

The equation is:

Equation 8.18. Equation for layer mode "Darken only"

$$E = \min(M, I)$$

The mode is commutative; the order of the two layers doesn't matter.

Lighten only

Figure 8.27. Example for layer mode "Lighten only"

Mask 1 is used as upper layer with 100% opacity.

Mask 2 is used as upper layer with 100% opacity.

Lighten only mode compares each component of each pixel in the upper layer with the corresponding one in the lower layer and uses the larger value in the resulting image. Completely black layers have no effect on the final image and completely white layers result in a white image.

The equation is:

Equation 8.19. Equation for layer mode "Lighten only"

$$E = \max(M, I)$$

The mode is commutative; the order of the two layers doesn't matter.

Hue

Figure 8.28. Example for layer mode "Hue"

Mask 1 is used as upper layer with 100% opacity.

Mask 2 is used as upper layer with 100% opacity.

Hue mode uses the hue of the upper layer and the saturation and value of the lower layer to form the resulting image. However, if the saturation of the upper layer is zero, the hue is taken from the lower layer, too.

Saturation

Figure 8.29. Example for layer mode "Saturation"

Mask 1 is used as upper layer with 100% opacity.

Mask 2 is used as upper layer with 100% opacity.

Saturation mode uses the saturation of the upper layer and the hue and value of the lower layer to form the resulting image.

Color

Figure 8.30. Example for layer mode "Color"

Mask 1 is used as upper layer with 100% opacity.

Mask 2 is used as upper layer with 100% opacity.

Color mode uses the hue and saturation of the upper layer and the value of the lower layer to form the resulting image.

Value

Figure 8.31. Example for layer mode "Value"

Mask 1 is used as upper layer with 100% opacity.

Mask 2 is used as upper layer with 100% opacity.

Value mode uses the value of the upper layer and the saturation and hue of the lower layer to form the resulting image. You can use this mode to reveal details in dark and light areas of an image without changing the saturation.

Each layer in an image can have a different layer mode. (Of course, the layer mode of the bottom layer of an image has no effect.) The effects of these layer modes are cumulative. The image shown below has three layers. The top layer consists of Wilber surrounded by transparency and has a layer mode of "Difference". The second layer is solid light blue and has a layer mode of "Addition". The bottom layer is filled with the "Red Cubes" pattern.

Figure 8.32. Multi layer example

GIMP also has similar modes which are used for the painting tools. These are the same twenty-one modes as the layer modes, plus additionally two modes which are specific to the painting tools. You can set these modes from the Mode menu in the Tools option dialog. In the equations shown above, the layer you are painting on is the "lower layer" and the pixels painted by the tool are the "upper layer". Naturally, you do not need more than one layer in the image to use these modes, since they only operate on the current layer and the selected painting tool.

See **Section 3.1.3, "Paint Mode Examples"** for a description of the two additional painting modes.

The equation is the *theoretical* equation. Due to **Bug #162395** , the actual equation is equivalent to Soft light. It is difficult to fix this bug without changing the appearance of existing images.

3. Creating New Layers

There are several ways to create new layers in an image. Here are the most important ones:

- Selecting Layer → New Layer in the image menu. This brings up a dialog that allows you to set the basic properties of the new layer; see the **New Layer dialog** section for help with it.
- Selecting Layer → Duplicate Layer in the image menu. This creates a new layer, that is a perfect copy of the currently active layer, just above the active layer.

- When you "cut" or "copy" something, and then paste it using **Ctrl+V** or Edit → Paste, the result is a "floating selection", which is a sort of temporary layer. Before you can do anything else, you either have to anchor the floating selection to an existing layer, or convert it into a normal layer. If you do the latter, the new layer will be sized just large enough to contain the pasted material.

4. Layer Groups

This possibility appeared with GIMP-2.8.

You can group layers that have similarities in a tree-like way. So, the layer list becomes easier to manage.

Create a Layer Group

>You can create a layer group by clicking on the Create a new layer group button at the bottom of the layer dialog,
>
>through Layer → New Layer Group, or through the layer dialog context menu.
>
>This empty layer group appears just above the current layer. It is important to give it an evocative name (double-click or **F2** on the

182

name, or use **Edit Layer Attributes** in the context menu you get by right clicking the Layer dialog, to edit it), else you will get confused when several ones are created.

You can create several layer groups and you can **embed** them, that is include a layer group in another one.

Adding Layers to a Layer Group

You can add *existing layers* to a layer group by click-and-dragging them.

Note

The hand representing the mouse pointer must turn smaller before releasing the mouse button.

A thin horizontal line marks where the layer will be laid down.

To add a *new layer* to the current layer group, click on the Create a new layer at the bottom of the layer dialog, or use the New Layer command in the image menu.

When a layer group is not empty, a small ">" icon appears. By clicking on it, you can fold/unfold the layer list.

You can put layers to be added together to a layer group by making them, them only, visible, and using the "New From Visible " command. All visible layers, outside and inside layer groups, will be added to the active layer group.

Layers that belong to a layer group are slightly indented to the right, allowing you know easily which layers are part of the group.

Raise and Lower Layer Groups

You can raise and lower layer groups in the layer dialog as you do with normal layers: click-and-dragging, using arrow up and down keys at the bottom of the layer dialog.

Duplicate a Layer Group

> You can duplicate a layer group: click on the Create a duplicate of the layer button or right-click and select the **Duplicate Layer** command in the pop up context menu.

Move Layer Groups

> You can **move a layer group to another image** by click-and-dragging. You can also copy-paste it using Ctrl-C and Ctrl-V: then, you get a floating selection that you must anchor (anchor button at the bottom of the layer dialog).
>
> You can also **move a layer group to the canvas**: this duplicates the group *in* the group. Chain all layers in the duplicated layer group, activate the Move tool, then, in the image, move the layer. That's a way to multiply multi-layer objects in an image.

Delete a Layer Group

> To delete a layer group, click on the red cross button at the bottom of the layer dialog or right-click and select **Delete layer**.

Embed Layer Groups

> When a layer group is activated, you can add another group inside it with the "Add New Layer Group" command. There seems to be no limit, excepted memory, to the number of embedded layer groups.

Layer Modes and Groups

> A layer mode applied to a layer group acts on layers that are in this group only. A layer mode above a layer group acts on all layers underneath, outside and inside the layer groups.

Original image

Figure 8.33. Layer Mode in or out Layer Group

We added a white layer *in* the layer group with saturation mode: only square and triangle are grayed out.

We added a white layer *out* of the layer group with saturation mode: all layers underneath are grayed out, background layer also.

Opacity

> When a layer group is activated, opacity changes are applied to all the layers of the group.

Layer Mask

> You cannot add a layer mask to a layer group (the corresponding option is grayed out). But, as with normal layers, you can add a layer mask to a layer in the group to mask a part of the layer.

We added a white (Full opacity) layer mask to the triangle layer.

Chapter 9. Text Management

1. Text Management

Text is managed with the Text tool. This tool creates a new layer containing the text, above the current layer in the layer dialog, with the size of the text box. Its name is the beginning of the text.

Figure 9.1. Example of a text item

Example of a text item, showing the boundary of the text layer. (Font: Utopia Bold)

The layer dialog, with the text layer above the layer which was current.

The Text tool is progressively improved. With GIMP-2.8, you can now edit text directly on canvas. A text tool box has been added which overlays the canvas above the text box.

As soon as you click on the canvas with the Text tool, you get a closed text box and a semi-transparent tool box just above.

Text tool options are described in **Section 6.6, "Text"**.

The default box mode is "Dynamic", and you can start typing text at once. The text box will enlarge gradually. Press **Enter** to add a new line.

You can also **enlarge the text box** by click-and-dragging, as you do with selections. Note that box mode turns to "Fixed". You also have to press **Enter** to add a new line.

To **edit text**, you must, first, select the part you want to edit by click-and-drag, or **Shift**+**arrow key** and then use the options of the **Section 2, "Text Tool Box"**.

Instead of using the on-canvas text editing, you can use the text editor dialog described in **Section 6.6.4, "Text Editor"**.

You can **move the text** on the image using the Move tool: you must click on a character, not on the background.

You can get **Unicode characters** with **Ctrl**+**Shift**+**U** plus hexadecimal Unicode code of the desired char. Please see **Section 6.6.4, "Text Editor"**.

You can **edit the text later**, if the text layer still exists and has not been modified by another tool (see below): make the text layer active in the **Layer dialog,** select the Text tool and click on the text in the image window.

Managing Text Layer

> You can operate on a text layer in the same ways as any other layer, but doing so often means giving up the ability to edit the text without losing the results of your work.
>
> To understand some of the idiosyncrasies of text handling, it may help for you to realize that a text layer contains more information than the pixel data that you see: it also contains a representation of the text in a text-editor format. You can see this in the text-editor window that pops up while you are using the Text tool. Every time you alter the text, the image layer is redrawn to reflect your changes.
>
> Now suppose you create a text layer, and then operate on it in some way that does not involve the Text tool: rotate it, for example. Suppose you then come back and try to edit it using the Text tool. As soon as you edit the text, the Text tool will redraw the layer, wiping out the results of the operations you performed in the meantime.

Because this danger is not obvious, the Text tool tries to protect you from it. If you operate on a text layer, and then later try to edit the text, a message pops up, warning you that your alterations will be undone, and giving you three options:

- edit the text anyway;
- cancel;
- create a new text layer with the same text as the existing layer, leaving the existing layer unchanged.

Figure 9.2. Warning lose modifications

Text Editing Context Menu

Figure 9.3. Text Editing Context Menu

You get this menu by right-clicking on text. It is somewhat different from that of the Text Editor dialog.

- Cut, Copy, Paste, Delete: these options concern a selected text. They remain grayed out as long as no text is selected. "Paste" is activated if the clipboard is full of text.
- Open text file: this command opens a file browser where you can find the wanted text file.
- Clear: this command deletes all the text, selected or not.
- Path from text: this command creates a path from the outlines of the current text. The result is not evident. You have to open the Path dialog and make path visible. Then select the Path tool and click on the text. Every letter is now surrounded with a path component. So you can modify the shape of letters by moving path control points.

  This command is similar to Layer → Text to Path.

- Text along path:

  This option is enabled only if a path exists. When your text is created, then create or import a path and make it active. If you create your path before the text, the path becomes invisible and you have to make it visible in the Path Dialog.

  This command is also available from the "Layer" menu:

Figure 9.4. The Text along Path command among text commands in the Layer menu

This group of options appears only if a text layer exists.

Click on the Text along Path button. The text is bent along the path. Letters are represented with their outline. Each of them is a component of the new path that appears in the Path dialog. All path options should apply to this new path.

Figure 9.5. "Text along Path" example

- From Left to Right / From Right to Left: fix the writing direction of your language.
- Input Methods: methods are available for some languages. For example, selecting "Inuktitut" transforms your keyboard into an Inuktitut keyboard, temporarily.

2. Text Tool Box

Figure 9.6. Text Tool Box

You get this box, which overlays canvas, as soon as you click on canvas with the Text Tool. It allows you to edit text directly on canvas.

Apart from the usual text formatting features like font family, style and size selectors you get numeric control over baseline offset and kerning, as well as the ability to change text color for a selection.

Help pop-ups are self-explanatory.

You can also use **Alt+Arrow keys** to change baseline offset and kerning.

> **Important**
>
> These features work on selected text. You get weird effects if no text is selected.

2.1. Text Tool Box Context menu

TODO

3. Text

3.1. Embellishing Text

Figure 9.7. Fancy text

Four fancy text items created using logo scripts: "alien neon", "bovination", "frosty", and "chalk". Default settings were used for everything except font size.

There are many things you can do to vary the appearance of text beyond just rendering it with different fonts or different colors. By converting a text item to a selection or a path, you can fill it, stroke the outlines, transform it, or generally apply the whole panoply of GIMP tools to get interesting effects. As a demonstration of some of the possibilities, try out the "logo" scripts at File → Create → Logos. Each of these scripts allows you to enter some text, and then creates a new image showing a logo constructed out of that text. If you would like to modify one of these scripts, or construct a logo script of your own, the Using Script-Fu and Script-Fu Tutorial sections should help you get started. Of course, you don't need Script-Fu to create these sorts of effects, only to automate them.

3.2. Adding Fonts

For the most authoritative and up-to-date information on fonts in GIMP, consult the "Fonts in GIMP 2.0" page GIMP-FONTS at the GIMP web site. This section attempts to give you a helpful overview.

GIMP uses the FreeType 2 font engine to render fonts, and a system called Fontconfig to manage them. GIMP will let you use any font in Fontconfig's font path; it will also let you use any font it finds in GIMP's font search path, which is set on the Font Folders page of the Preferences dialog. By default, the font search path includes a system GIMP-fonts folder (which you should not alter, even though it is actually empty), and a fonts folder inside your personal GIMP directory. You can add new folders to the font search path if it is more convenient for you.

FreeType 2 is a very powerful and flexible system. By default, it supports the following font file formats:

- TrueType fonts (and collections)
- Type 1 fonts
- CID-keyed Type 1 fonts
- CFF fonts
- OpenType fonts (both TrueType and CFF variants)
- SFNT-based bitmap fonts
- X11 PCF fonts
- Windows FNT fonts
- BDF fonts (including anti-aliased ones)
- PFR fonts
- Type42 fonts (limited support)

You can also add modules to support other types of font files. See FREETYPE 2 FREETYPE for more information.

Linux. On a Linux system, if the Fontconfig utility is set up as usual, all you need to do to add a new font is to place the file in the directory ~/.fonts. This will make the font available not only to GIMP, but to any other program that uses Fontconfig. If for some reason you want the font to be available to GIMP only, you can place it in the fonts sub-directory of your personal GIMP directory, or some other location in your font search path. Doing either will cause the font to show up the next time you start GIMP. If you want to use it in an already running GIMP, press the *Refresh* button in the Fonts dialog.

Windows. The easiest way to install a font is to drag the file onto the Fonts directory and let the shell do its magic. Unless you've done something creative, it's probably in its default location of C:\windows\fonts or C:\winnt\fonts. Sometimes double-clicking on a font will install it as well as display it; sometimes it only displays it. This method will make the font available not only to GIMP, but also to other Windows applications.

Mac OS X. There are several ways to install fonts on your system. You can drag-and-drop them to the "Fonts" folder in "Libraries" folder of your "Home Folder". Or you may use Font Book, invoked by double-clicking the font file icon in the Finder. You can see what the font looks like, and click your favorite fonts so that their files are to be installed on the system. These methods will make the fonts available for all applications, not only GIMP. If you want all users can use the fonts, drag-and-drop the fonts to the "Fonts" folder in "Libraries" folder of the Mac OS X™ Disk, or to the "Computer" folder in the Collection column of Font Book.

To install a Type 1 file, you need both the .pfb and .pfm files. Drag the one that gets an icon into the fonts folder. The other one doesn't strictly need to be in the same directory when you drag the file, since it uses some kind of search algorithm to find it if it's not, but in any case putting it in the same directory does no harm.

In principle, GIMP can use any type of font on Windows that FreeType can handle; however, for fonts that Windows can't handle natively, you should install them by placing the font files in the fonts folder of your personal GIMP directory, or some other location in your font search path. The support Windows has varies by version. All that GIMP runs on support at least TrueType, Windows FON, and Windows FNT. Windows 2000 and later support Type 1 and OpenType. Windows ME supports OpenType and possibly Type 1 (but the most widely used Windows GIMP installer does not officially support Windows ME, although it may work anyway).

> **Note**
>
> GIMP uses Fontconfig to manage fonts on Windows as well as Linux. The instructions above work because Fontconfig by default uses the Windows fonts directory, i. e., the same fonts that Windows uses itself. If for some reason your Fontconfig is set up differently, you will have to figure out where to put fonts so that GIMP can find them: in any case, the fonts folder of your personal GIMP directory should work.

3.3. Font Problems

Problems with fonts have probably been responsible for more GIMP 2 bug reports than any other single cause, although they have become much less frequent in the most recent releases in the 2.0 series. In most cases they have been caused by malformed font files giving trouble to Fontconfig. If you experience crashes at start-up when GIMP scans your font directories, the best solution is to upgrade to a version of Fontconfig newer than 2.2.0. As a quick workaround you can start gimp with the --no-fonts command-line option, but then you will not be able to use the text tool.

Another known problem is that Pango 1.2 cannot load fonts that don't provide an Unicode character mapping. (Pango is the text layout library used by GIMP.) A lot of symbol fonts fall into this category. On some systems, using such a font can cause GIMP to crash. Updating to Pango 1.4 will fix this problem and makes symbol fonts available in GIMP.

A frequent source of confusion occurs on Windows systems, when GIMP encounters a malformed font file and generates an error message: this causes a console window to pop up so that you can see the message. *Do not close that console window. It is harmless, and closing it will shut down GIMP.* When this happens, it often seems to users that GIMP has crashed. It hasn't: closing the console window causes Windows to shut GIMP down. Unfortunately, this annoying situation is caused by an interaction between Windows and the libraries that GIMP links to: it cannot be fixed within GIMP. All you need to do, though, if this happens, is minimize the console window and ignore it.

Chapter 10. Enhancing Photographs

1. Working with Digital Camera Photos

1.1. Introduction

One of the most common uses of GIMP is to fix digital camera images that for some reason are less than perfect. Maybe the image is overexposed or underexposed; maybe rotated a bit; maybe out of focus: these are all common problems for which GIMP has good tools. The purpose of this chapter is to give you an overview of those tools and the situations in which they are useful. You will not find detailed tutorials here: in most cases it is easier to learn how to use the tools by experimenting with them than by reading about them. (Also, each tool is described more thoroughly in the Help section devoted to it.) You will also not find anything in this chapter about the multitude of "special effects" that you can apply to an image using GIMP. You should be familiar with basic GIMP concepts before reading this chapter, but you certainly don't need to be an expert–if you are, you probably know most of this anyway. And don't hesitate to experiment: GIMP's powerful "undo" system allows you to recover from almost any mistake with a simple **Ctrl+Z**.

Most commonly the things that you want to do to clean up an imperfect photo are of four types: improving the composition; improving the colors; improving the sharpness; and removing artifacts or other undesirable elements of the image.

1.2. Improving Composition
1.2.1. Rotating an Image

It is easy, when taking a picture, to hold the camera not quite perfectly vertical, resulting in a picture where things are tilted at an angle. In GIMP, the way to fix this is to use the Rotate tool. Activate this by clicking its icon in the Toolbox, or by pressing the **Shift+R** while inside the image. Make sure the Tool Options are visible, and at the top, make sure for "Transform:" that the left button ("Transform Layer") is selected. If you then click the mouse inside the image and drag it, you will see a grid appear that rotates as you drag. When the grid looks right, click Rotate or press **Enter**, and the image will be rotated.

Now as a matter of fact, it isn't so easy to get things right by this method: you often find that things are better but not quite perfect. One solution is to rotate a bit more, but there is a disadvantage to that approach. Each time you rotate an image, because the rotated pixels don't line up precisely with the original pixels, the image inevitably gets blurred a little bit. For a single rotation, the amount of blurring is quite small, but two rotations cause twice as much blurring as one, and there is no reason to blur things more than you have to. A better alternative is to undo the rotation and then do another, adjusting the angle.

Fortunately, GIMP provides another way of doing it that is considerably easier to use: in the Rotate Tool Options, for the Transform Direction you can select "Backward (Corrective)". When you do this, instead of rotating the grid to compensate for the error, you can rotate it to *line up* with the error. If this seems confusing, try it and you will see that it is quite straightforward.

Note

Since GIMP 2.2, there is an option to preview the results of transformations, instead of just seeing a grid. This makes it easier to get things right on the first try.

After you have rotated an image, there will be unpleasant triangular "holes" at the corners. One way to fix them is to create a background that fills the holes with some unobtrusive or neutral color, but usually a better solution is to crop the image. The greater the rotation, the more cropping is required, so it is best to get the camera aligned as well as possible when you take the picture in the first place.

1.2.2. Cropping

When you take a picture with a digital camera, you have some control over what gets included in the image but often not as much as you would like: the result is images that could benefit from trimming. Beyond this, it is often possible to enhance the impact of an image by trimming it so that the most important elements are placed at key points. A rule of thumb, not always to be followed but good to keep in mind, is the "rule of thirds", which says that maximum impact is obtained by placing the center of interest one-third of the way across the image, both widthwise and heightwise.

To crop an image, activate the Crop tool in the Toolbox, or by pressing the "C" key (capitalized) while inside the image. With the tool active, clicking and dragging in the image will sweep out a crop rectangle. It will also pop up a dialog that allows you to adjust the dimensions of the crop region if they aren't quite right. When everything is perfect, hit the Crop button in the dialog.

1.3. Improving Colors

1.3.1. Automated Tools

In spite of sophisticated exposure-control systems, pictures taken with digital cameras often come out over- or under-exposed, or with color casts due to imperfections in lighting. GIMP gives you a variety of tools to correct colors in an image, ranging to automated tools that run with a simple button-click to highly sophisticated tools that give you many parameters of control. We will start with the simplest first.

GIMP gives you several automated color correction tools. Unfortunately they don't usually give you quite the results you are looking for, but they only take a moment to try out, and if nothing else they often give you an idea of some of the possibilities inherent in the image. Except for "Auto Levels", you can find these tools by following the menu path Colors → Auto in the image menu.

Here they are, with a few words about each:

Normalize

> This tool (it is really a plug-in) is useful for underexposed images: it adjusts the whole image uniformly until the brightest point is right at the saturation limit, and the darkest point is black. The downside is that the amount of brightening is determined entirely by the lightest and darkest points in the image, so even one single white pixel and/or one single black pixel will make normalization ineffective.

Equalize

> This is a very powerful adjustment that tries to spread the colors in the image evenly across the range of possible intensities. In some cases the effect is amazing, bringing out contrasts that are very difficult to get in any other way; but more commonly, it just makes the image look weird. Oh well, it only takes a moment to try.

Color Enhance

> This command increases the saturation range of the colors in the layer, without altering brightness or hue. So this command does not work on grayscale images.

Stretch Contrast

This is like "Normalize", except that it operates on the red, green, and blue channels independently. It often has the useful effect of reducing color casts.

Stretch HSV

Does the same as Stretch Contrast but works in HSV color space, rather than RGB color space. It preserves the Hue.

White balance

This may enhance images with poor white or black by removing little used colors and stretch the remaining range as much as possible.

Auto Levels

This is done by activating the Levels tool (Tools → Color Tools → Levels or Colors → Levels in the image menu), and then pressing the Auto button near the center of the dialog. You will see a preview of the result; you must press Okay for it to take effect. Pressing Cancel instead will cause your image to revert to its previous state.

If you can find a point in the image that ought to be perfect white, and a second point that ought to be perfect black, then you can use the Levels tool to do a semi-automatic adjustment that will often do a good job of fixing both brightness and colors throughout the image. First, bring up the Levels tool as previously described. Now, look down near the bottom of the Layers dialog for three buttons with symbols on them that look like eye-droppers (at least, that is what they are supposed to look like). The one on the left, if you mouse over it, shows its function to be "Pick Black Point". Click on this, then click on a point in the image that ought to be black–really truly perfectly black, not just sort of dark–and watch the image change. Next, click on the rightmost of the three buttons ("Pick White Point"), and then click a point in the image that ought to be white, and once more watch the image change. If you are happy with the result, click the Okay button otherwise Cancel.

Those are the automated color adjustments: if you find that none of them quite does the job for you, it is time to try one of the interactive color tools. All of these, except one, can be accessed via Tools->Color Tools in the image menu. After you select a color tool, click on the image (anywhere) to activate it and bring up its dialog.

1.3.2. Exposure Problems

The simplest tool to use is the Brightness/Contrast tool. It is also the least powerful, but in many cases it does everything you need. This tool is often useful for images that are overexposed or underexposed; it is not useful for correcting color casts. The tool gives you two sliders to adjust, for "Brightness" and "Contrast". If you have the option "Preview" checked (and almost certainly you should),you will see any adjustments you make reflected in the image. When you are happy with the results, press Okay and they will take effect. If you can't get results that you are happy with, press Cancel and the image will revert to its previous state.

A more sophisticated, and only slightly more difficult, way of correcting exposure problems is to use the Levels tool. The dialog for this tool looks very complicated, but for the basic usage we have in mind here, the only part you need to deal with is the "Input Levels" area, specifically the three triangular sliders that appear below the histogram. We refer you to the Levels Tool Help for instructions; but actually the easiest way to learn how to use it is to experiment by moving the three sliders around, and watching how the image is affected. (Make sure that "Preview" is checked at the bottom of the dialog.)

A very powerful way of correcting exposure problems is to use the *Curves* tool. This tool allows you to click and drag control points on a curve, in order to create a function mapping input brightness levels to output brightness levels. The Curves tool can replicate any effect you can achieve with Brightness/Contrast or the Levels tool, so it is more powerful than either of them. Once again, we refer you to the Curves Tool Help for detailed instructions, but the easiest way to learn how to use it is by experimenting.

The most powerful approach to adjusting brightness and contrast across an image, for more expert GIMP users, is to create a new layer above the one you are working on, and then in the Layers dialog set the Mode for the upper layer to "Multiply". The new layer then serves as a "gain control" layer for the layer below it, with white yielding maximum gain and black yielding a gain of zero. Thus, by painting on the new layer, you can selectively adjust the gain for each area of the image, giving you very fine control. You should try to paint only with smooth gradients, because sudden changes in gain will give rise to spurious edges in the result. Paint only using shades of gray, not colors, unless you want to produce color shifts in the image.

Actually, "Multiply" is not the only mode that is useful for gain control. In fact, "Multiply" mode can only darken parts of an image, never lighten them, so it is only useful where some parts of an image are overexposed. Using "Divide" mode has the opposite effect: it can brighten areas of an image but not darken them. Here is a trick that is often useful for bringing out the maximum amount of detail across all areas of an image:

1. Duplicate the layer (producing a new layer above it).
2. Desaturate the new layer.
3. Apply a Gaussian blur to the result, with a large radius (100 or more).
4. Set Mode in the Layers dialog to Divide.
5. Control the amount of correction by adjusting opacity in the Layers dialog, or by using Brightness/Contrast, Levels, or Curves tools on the new layer.
6. When you are happy with the result, you can use Merge Down to combine the control layer and the original layer into a single layer.

In addition to "Multiply" and "Divide", you may every so often get useful effects with other layer combination modes, such as "Dodge", "Burn", or "Soft Light". It is all too easy, though, once you start playing with these things, to look away from the computer for a moment and suddenly find that you have just spent an hour twiddling parameters. Be warned: the more options you have, the harder it is to make a decision.

1.3.3. Adjusting Hue and Saturation

In our experience, if your image has a color cast---too much red, too much blue, etc---the easiest way to correct it is to use the Levels tool, adjusting levels individually on the red, green, and blue channels. If this doesn't work for you, it might be worth your while to try the Color Balance tool or the Curves tool, but these are much more difficult to use effectively. (They are very good for creating certain types of special effects, though.)

Sometimes it is hard to tell whether you have adjusted colors adequately. A good, objective technique is to find a point in the image that you know should be either white or a shade of gray. Activate the Color Picker tool (the eyedropper symbol in the Toolbox), and click on the aforesaid point: this brings up the Color Picker dialog. If the colors are correctly adjusted, then the red, green, and blue components of the reported color should all be equal; if not, then you should see what sort of adjustment you need to make. This technique, when well used, allows even color-blind people to color-correct an image.

If your image is washed out---which can easily happen when you take pictures in bright light---try the Hue/Saturation tool, which gives you three sliders to manipulate, for Hue, Lightness, and Saturation. Raising the saturation will probably make the image look better. In same cases it is useful to adjust the lightness at the same time. ("Lightness" here is similar to "Brightness" in the Brightness/Contrast tool, except that they are formed from different combinations of the red, green, and blue channels.) The Hue/Saturation tool gives you the option of adjusting restricted subranges of colors (using the buttons at the top of the dialog), but if you want to get natural-looking colors, in most cases you should avoid doing this.

> **Tip**
>
> Even if an image does not seemed washed out, often you can increase its impact by pushing up the saturation a bit. Veterans of the film era sometimes call this trick "Fujifying", after Fujichrome film, which is notorious for producing highly saturated prints.

When you take pictures in low light conditions, in some cases you have the opposite problem: too much saturation. In this case too the Hue/Saturation tool is a good one to use, only by reducing the saturation instead of increasing it.

1.4. Adjusting Sharpness
1.4.1. Unblurring

If the focus on the camera is not set perfectly, or the camera is moving when the picture is taken, the result is a blurred image. If there is a lot of blurring, you probably won't be able to do much about it with any technique, but if there is only a moderate amount, you should be able to improve the image.

The most generally useful technique for sharpening a fuzzy image is called the Unsharp Mask. In spite of the rather confusing name, which derives from its origins as a technique used by film developers, its result is to make the image sharper, not "unsharp". It is a plug-in, and you can access it as Filters->Enhance->Unsharp Mask in the image menu. There are two parameters, "Radius" and "Amount". The default values often work pretty well, so you should try them first. Increasing either the radius or the amount increases the strength of the effect. Don't get carried away, though: if you make the unsharp mask too strong, it will amplify noise in the image and also give rise to visible artifacts where there are sharp edges.

> **Tip**
>
> Sometimes using Unsharp Mask can cause color distortion where there are strong contrasts in an image. When this happens, you can often get better results by decomposing the image into separate Hue-Saturation-Value (HSV) layers, and running Unsharp Mask on the Value layer only, then recomposing. This works because the human eye has much finer resolution for brightness than for color. See the sections on **Decompose** and **Compose** for more information.

Next to "Unsharp Mask" in the Filters menu is another filter called Sharpen, which does similar things. It is a little easier to use but not nearly as effective: our recommendation is that you ignore it and go straight to Unsharp Mask.

In some situations, you may be able to get useful results by selectively sharpening specific parts of an image using the Blur or Sharpen tool from the Toolbox, in "Sharpen" mode. This allows you to increase the sharpness in areas by painting over them with any paintbrush. You should be restrained about this, though, or the results will not look very natural: sharpening increases the apparent sharpness of edges in the image, but also amplifies noise.

1.4.2. Reducing Graininess

When you take pictures in low-light conditions or with a very fast exposure time, the camera does not get enough data to make good estimates of the true color at each pixel, and consequently the resulting image looks grainy. You can "smooth out" the graininess by blurring the image, but then you will also lose sharpness. There are a couple of approaches that may give better results. Probably the best, if the graininess is not too bad, is to use the filter called Selective Blur, setting the blurring radius to 1 or 2 pixels. The other approach is to use the Despeckle filter. This has a nice preview, so you can play with the settings and try to find some that give good results. When graininess is really bad, though, it is often very difficult to fix by anything except heroic measures (i.e., retouching with paint tools).

1.4.3. Softening

Every so often you have the opposite problem: an image is *too* crisp. The solution is to blur it a bit: fortunately blurring an image is much easier than sharpening it. Since you probably don't want to blur it very much, the simplest method is to use the "Blur" plug-in, accessed via Filters->Blur->Blur from the image menu. This will soften the focus of the image a little bit. If you want more softening, just repeat until you get the result you desire.

1.5. Removing Unwanted Objects from an Image

There are two kinds of objects you might want to remove from an image: first, artifacts caused by junk such as dust or hair on the lens; second, things that were really present but impair the quality of the image, such as a telephone wire running across the edge of a beautiful mountain landscape.

1.5.1. Despeckling

A good tool for removing dust and other types of lens grunge is the Despeckle filter, accessed as Filters->Enhance->Despeckle from the image menu. Very important: to use this filter effectively, you must begin by making a small selection containing the artifact and a small area around it. The selection must be small enough so that the artifact pixels are statistically distinguishable from the other pixels inside the selection. If you try to run despeckle on the whole image, you will hardly ever get anything useful. Once you have created a reasonable selection, activate Despeckle, and watch the preview as you adjust the parameters. If you are lucky, you will be able to find a setting that removes the junk while minimally affecting the area around it. The more the junk stands out from the area around it, the better your results are likely to be. If it isn't working for you, it might be worthwhile to cancel the filter, create a different selection, and then try again.

If you have more than one artifact in the image, it is necessary to use Despeckle on each individually.

1.5.2. Garbage Removal

The most useful method for removing unwanted "clutter" from an image is the Clone tool, which allows you to paint over one part of an image using pixel data taken from another part (or even from a different image). The trick to using the clone tool effectively is to be able to find a different part of the image that can be used to "copy over" the unwanted part: if the area surrounding the unwanted object is very different from the rest of the image, you won't have much luck. For example, if you have a lovely beach scene, with a nasty human walking across the beach who you would like to teleport away, you will probably be able to find an empty part of the beach that looks similar to the part he is walking across, and use it to clone over him. It is quite astonishing how natural the results can look when this technique works well.

Consult the Clone Tool Help for more detailed instructions. Cloning is as much an art as a science, and the more you practice at it, the better you will get. At first it may seem impossible to produce anything except ugly blotches, but persistence will pay off.

Another tool looking very much as the clone tool, but smarter, is the **healing tool w**hich also takes the area around the destination into account when cloning. A typical usage is removal of wrinkles and other minor errors in images.

In some cases you may be able to get good results by simply cutting out the offending object from the image, and then using a plug-in called

"Resynthesizer" to fill in the void. This plug-in is not included with the main GIMP distribution, but it can be obtained from the author's web site [PLUGIN-RESYNTH]. As with many things, your mileage may vary.

1.5.3. Removing Red-eye

When you take a flash picture of somebody who is looking directly toward the camera, the iris of the eye can bounce the light of the flash back toward the camera in such a way as to make the eye appear bright red: this effect is called "red eye", and looks very bizarre. Many modern cameras have special flash modes that minimize red-eye, but they only work if you use them, and even then they don't always work perfectly. Interestingly, the same effect occurs with animals, but the eyes may show up as other colors, such as green.

From version 2.4, GIMP incorporated a special remove red eye filter. Make a selection with one of the selection tools of the red part of the eye and then choose the "Remove Red Eye" filter. Perhaps you have to fiddle around a bit with the threshold slider to get the right color.

1.6. Saving Your Results
1.6.1. Files

What file format should you use to save the results of your work, and should you resize it? The answers depend on what you intend to use the image for.

- If you intend to open the image in GIMP again for further work, you should save it in GIMP's native XCF format (i. e., name it something.xcf), because this is the only format that guarantees that none of the information in the image is lost.
- If you intend to print the image on paper, you should avoid shrinking the image, except by cropping it. The reason is that printers are capable of achieving much higher resolutions than video monitors — 600 to 1400 dpi ("dots per inch", the physical density) for typical printers, as compared to 72 to 100 pixels per inch for monitors. A 3000 x 5000-pixel image looks huge on a monitor, but it only comes to about 5 inches by 8 inches on paper at 600 ppi. There is usually no good reason to *expand* the image either: you can't increase the true resolution that way, and it can always be scaled up at the time it is printed. As for the file format, it will usually be fine to use JPEG at a quality level of 75 to 85. In rare cases, where there are large swaths of nearly uniform color, you may need to set the quality level even higher or use a lossless format such as TIFF instead.
- If you intend to display the image on screen or project it with a video projector, bear in mind that the highest screen resolution for most commonly available systems is 1600 x 1200, so there is nothing to gain

by keeping the image larger than that. For this purpose, the JPEG format is almost always a good choice.
- If you want to put the image on a web page or send it by email, it is a good idea to make every effort to keep the file size as small as possible. First, scale the image down to the smallest size that makes it possible to see the relevant details (bear in mind that other people may be using different sized monitors and/or different monitor resolution settings). Second, save the image as a JPEG file. In the JPEG save dialog, check the option to "Preview in image window" , and then adjust the Quality slider to the lowest level that gives you acceptable image quality. (You will see in the image the effects of each change.) Make sure that the image is zoomed at 1:1 while you do this, so you are not misled by the effects of zooming.

See the **File Formats** section for more information.

1.6.2. Printing Your Photos

As in most softwares, in GIMP, printing needs to go to main menu File → Print. However it is very useful to keep in mind some elementary concepts to prevent some unpleasant surprises when looking at result, or to cure them if that occurs. You always must remember:

- that image displayed on the screen is in RGB mode and printing will be in CMYK mode; consequently color feature you'll get on printed sheet will not be exactly what you was waiting for. That depends on the used corresponding chart. For the curious ones some adding explanations can be got through a click on these useful Wikipedia links:
    - ICC-Profile [WKPD-ICC]
    - CMYK [WKPD-CMYK]
    - Gamut [WKPD-GAMUT]
- that a screen resolution is roughly within a range from 75 up to 100 dpi; a printer resolution is about 10x higher (or more) than a screen one; printed image size depends on available pixels and resolution; so actual printed size doesn't correspond inevitably to what is displayed on screen nor available sheet size.

Consequently, before any printing it is relevant to go to: Image → Print size and choose here your convenient output size in "print size" box adjusting either sizes or resolution. The symbol shows that the both values are linked. You can dissociate x and y resolution by clicking on that symbol, but it is risky! Probably this possibility is open because printers are built with different x vs. y resolutions. Nevertheless if you unlinked them you can be very surprised! You can try this in special effects.

Last recommendation: think of checking your margins as well as centering. It would be a pity if a too much large margin cuts off some part of your image or if an inappropriate centering damages your work especially if you use a special photo paper.

1.6.3. EXIF Data

Modern digital cameras, when you take a picture, add information to the data file about the camera settings and the circumstances under which the picture was taken. This data is included in JPEG or TIFF files in a structured format called EXIF. For JPEG files, GIMP is capable of maintaining EXIF data, if it is built appropriately: it depends on a library called "libexif", which may not be available on all systems. If GIMP is built with EXIF support enabled, then loading a JPEG file with EXIF data, and resaving the resulting image in JPEG format, will cause the EXIF data to be preserved unchanged. This is not, strictly speaking, the right way for an image editor to handle EXIF data, but it is better than simply removing it, which is what earlier versions of GIMP did.

If you would like to see the contents of the EXIF data, you can download from the registry an Exif Browser plug-in [PLUGIN-EXIF]. If you are able to build and install it on your system, you can access it as Filters->Generic->Exif Browser from the image menu. (See **Installing New Plug-ins** for help.)

Chapter 11. Color Management with GIMP

1. Color Management in GIMP

Many devices you use in your design or photography workflow, like digital photo cameras, scanners, displays, printers etc., have their own color reproduction characteristics. If those are not taken into account during opening, editing and saving, harmful adjustments can be done to images. With GIMP you can have reliable output for both Web and print.

Figure 11.1. Image Processing Workflow

Workflow without Color management

Process with Color management

1.1. Problems of a non Color Managed Workflow

The basic problem of image manipulation without color management is that you do simply not see what you do. This affects two different areas:

1. There are differences in Colors caused by different color characteristics of different devices like cameras, scanners, displays or printers
2. There are differences in Colors caused by the limitations of the colorspace a specific device is able to handle

The main purpose of color management is to avoid such problems. The approach taken to do so involves the addition of a description of the color characteristic to an image or devices.

These descriptions are called *color profile*. A color profile is basically a look-up table to translate the specific color characteristic of a device to a device-independent color space - the so called working-space. All the image manipulation is then done to images in the working-space. In addition to that the color profile of a device can be used to simulate how colors would look on that device.

The creation of color profiles is most often done by the manufacturer of the devices themselves. To make these profiles usable independent of platform and operating system, the ICC (International Color Consortium) created a standard called ICC-profile that describes how color profiles are stored to files and embedded into images.

1.2. Introduction to a Color Managed Workflow

Tip

Most of the parameters and profiles described here can be set in the GIMP preferences. Please see **Section 1.14, "Color Management"** for details.

1.2.1. Input

Most digital cameras embed a color profile to individual photo files without user interaction. Digital scanners usually come with a color profile, which they also attach to the scanned images.

Figure 11.2. Applying the ICC-profile

When opening an image with an embedded color profile, GIMP offers to convert the file to the RGB working color space. This is sRGB by default and it is recommended that all work is done in that color space. Should you however decide to keep the embedded color profile, the image will however still be displayed correctly.

In case for some reason a color profile is not embedded in the image and you know (or have a good guess) which one it should be, you can manually assign it to that image.

1.2.2. Display

For the best results, you need a color profile for your monitor. If a monitor profile is configured, either system-wide or in the Color Management section of the GIMP Preferences dialog, the image colors will be displayed most accurately.

One of the most important GIMP commands to work with color management is described in **Section 5.8, "Display Filters"**.

If you do not have a color profile for your monitor, you can create it using hardware calibration and measurement tools. On UNIX systems you will need Argyll Color Management System™ ARGYLLCMS and/or LProf™ LPROF to create color profiles.

1.2.2.1. Display Calibration and Profiling

For displays there are two steps involved. One is called calibration and the other is called profiling. Also, calibration generally involves two steps. The first involves adjusting external monitor controls such as Contrast, Brightness, Color Temperature, etc, and it is highly dependent on the specific monitor. In addition there are further adjustments that are loaded into the video card memory to bring the monitor as close to a standard state as possible. This information is stored in the monitor profile in the so-called vgct tag. Probably under Windows XP or Mac OS, the operating system loads this information (LUT) in the video card in the process of starting your computer. Under Linux, at present you have to use an external program such as xcalib or dispwin. (If one just does a simple visual calibration using a web site such as that of Norman Koren, one might only use xgamma to load a gamma value.)

The second step, profiling, derives a set of rules which allow GIMP to translate RGB values in the image file into appropriate colors on the screen. This is also stored in the monitor profile. It doesn't change the RGB values in the image, but it does change which values are sent to the video card (which already contains the vgct LUT).

1.2.3. Print Simulation

Using GIMP, you can easily get a preview of what your image will look like on paper. Given a color profile for your printer, the display can be switched into Soft Proof mode. In such a simulated printout, colors that cannot be reproduced will optionally be marked with neutral gray color, allowing you to correct such mistakes before sending your images to the printer.

Chapter 12. Enrich my GIMP

1. Preferences Dialog

1.1. Introduction

Figure 12.1. List of preference pages

The preferences dialog can be accessed from the image menu-bar, through Edit → Preferences. It lets you customize many aspects of the way GIMP works. The following sections detail the settings that you can customize, and what they affect.

All of the Preferences information is stored in a file called gimprc in your personal GIMP directory, so if you are a "power user" who would rather work with a text editor than a graphical interface, you can alter preferences by editing that file. If you do, and you are on a Linux system, then **man gimprc** will give you a lot of technical information about the contents of the file and what they are used for.

1.2. Environment

Figure 12.2. Environment Preferences

This page lets you customize the amount of system memory allocated for various purposes. It also allows you to disable the confirmation dialogs that appear when you close unsaved images, and to set the size of thumbnail files that GIMP produces.

1.2.1. Options

Resource Consumption

Minimal number of undo levels

> GIMP allows you to undo most actions by maintaining an "Undo History" for each image, for which a certain amount of memory is allocated. Regardless of memory usage, however, GIMP always

permits some minimal number of the most recent actions to be undone: this is the number specified here. See **Section 3, "Undoing"** for more information about GIMP's Undo mechanism.

Maximum undo memory

> This is the amount of undo memory allocated for each image. If the Undo History size exceeds this, the oldest points are deleted, unless this would result in fewer points being present than the minimal number specified above.

Tile cache size

> This is the amount of system RAM allocated for GIMP image data. If GIMP requires more memory than this, it begins to swap to disk, which may in some circumstances cause a dramatic slowdown. You are given an opportunity to set this number when you install GIMP, but you can alter it here. See **How to Set Your Tile Cache** for more information.

Maximum new image size

> This is not a hard constraint: if you try to create a new image larger than the specified size, you are asked to confirm that you really want to do it. This is to prevent you from accidentally creating images much larger than you intend, which can either crash GIMP or cause it to respond verrrrrrrry slowwwwwwwwly.

Number of processors to use

> Default is one. Your computer may have more than one processor.

Image Thumbnails

Size of thumbnails

> This options allows you to set the size of the thumbnails shown in the File Open dialog (and also saved for possible use by other programs). The options are "None", "Normal (128x128)", and "Large (256x256)".

Maximum filesize for thumbnailing

> If an image file is larger than the specified maximum size, GIMP will not generate a thumbnail for it. This options allows you to prevent thumbnailing of extremely large image files from slowing GIMP to a crawl.

Saving Images

Confirm closing of unsaved images

> Closing an image is not undoable, so by default GIMP asks you to confirm that you really want to do it, whenever it would lead to a loss of unsaved changes. You can disable this if you find it annoying; but then of course you are responsible for remembering what you have and have not saved.

Document history

Keep record of used files in the Recent Documents list

> When checked, files you have opened will be saved in the Document history. You can access the list of files with the Document history dialog from the image menu-bar : File → Open Recent → Document History.

1.3. Interface

Figure 12.3. Assorted Interface Preferences

This page lets you customize language, layer/channel previews and keyboard shortcuts.

Options

Language

> The GIMP's default language is that of your system. You can select another language in the drop-down list. You have to start GIMP again to make this change effective. Please refer to **Section 1.2, "Language"**.

Previews

> By default, GIMP shows miniature previews of the contents of layers and channels in several places, including the Layers dialog. If for some reason you would prefer to disable these, you can do it by unchecking Enable layer and channel previews. If you do want previews to be shown, you can customize their sizes using the menus for Default layer and channel preview size and Navigation preview size.

Keyboard Shortcuts

> Any menu item can be activated by holding down **Alt** and pressing a sequence of keys. Normally, the key associated with each menu entry is shown as an underlined letter in the text, called *accelerator*. If for some reason you would prefer the underlines to go away (maybe because you think they're ugly and you don't use them anyway), then you can make this happen by unchecking Show menu mnemonics.

> GIMP can give you the ability to create keyboard shortcuts (key combinations that activate a menu entry) dynamically, by pressing the keys while the pointer hovers over the desired menu entry. However, this capability is disabled by default, because it might lead novice users to accidentally overwrite the standard keyboard shortcuts. If you want to enable it, check Use dynamics keyboard shortcuts here.

> Pressing the button for Configure Keyboard Shortcuts brings up the Shortcut Editor, which gives you a graphical interface to select menu items and assign shortcuts to them.

> If you change shortcuts, you will probably want your changes to continue to apply in future GIMP sessions. If not, uncheck Save keyboard shortcuts on exit. But remember that you have done this, or you may be frustrated later. If you don't want to save shortcuts on exit every session, you can save the current settings at any time using the

Save Keyboard Shortcuts Now button, and they will be applied to future sessions. If you decide that you have made some bad decisions concerning shortcuts, you can reset them to their original state by pressing Reset Saved Keyboard Shortcuts to Default Values.

1.4. Theme

Figure 12.4. Theme Preference

This page lets you select a theme, which determines many aspects of the appearance of the GIMP user interface, including the set of icons used, their sizes, fonts, spacing allowed in dialogs, etc. Two themes are supplied with GIMP: Default, which is probably best for most people, and Small, which may be preferable for those with small or low-resolution monitors. Clicking on a theme in the list causes it to be applied immediately, so it is easy to see the result and change your mind if you don't like it.

You can also use custom themes, either by downloading them from the net, or by copying one of the supplied themes and modifying it. Custom themes should be places in the themes subdirectory of your personal GIMP directory: if they are, they will appear in the list here. Each theme is actually a directory containing ASCII files that you can edit. They are pretty complicated, and the meaning of the contents goes beyond the scope of this documentation, but you should feel free to experiment: in the worst case, if you mess things up completely, you can always revert back to one of the supplied themes.

You cannot edit the supplied themes unless you have administrator permissions, and even if you do, you shouldn't: if you want to customize a theme, make a copy in your personal directory and work on it. If you make a change and would like to see the result "on the fly", you can do so by saving the edited theme file and then pressing Reload Current Theme.

1.5. Help System

Figure 12.5. Help System Preferences

This page lets you customize the behaviour of the GIMP help system.

1.5.1. Options

General

Show tool tips

> Tool tips are small help pop-ups that appear when the pointer hovers for a moment over some element of the interface, such as a button or icon. Sometimes they explain what the element does; sometimes they give you hints about non-obvious ways to use it. If you find them too distracting, you can disable them here by unchecking this option. We recommend that you leave them enabled unless you are a very advanced user.

Show help buttons

> This option controls whether the help buttons are shown on every tool dialog, which may be used alternatively to invoke the help system.

User manual

> This drop-down list lets you select between Use a locally installed copy and Use the online version. See **Section 12.2, "Help"**.

Help Browser

Help browser to use

> GIMP Help is supplied in the form of HTML files, i. e., web pages. You can view them using either a special help browser that comes with GIMP, or a web browser of your choice. Here you choose which option to use. Because the help pages were carefully checked to make sure they work well with GIMP's browser, whereas other web browsers are somewhat variable in their support of features, the safer option is to use the internal browser; but really any modern web browser should be okay.
>
> **Note**
>
> Note that the GIMP help browser is not available on all platforms. If it is missing, this option is hidden and the standard web browser will be used to read the help pages.

1.6. Tool Options

Figure 12.6. Tool Options Preferences

This page lets you customize several aspects of the behavior of tools.

1.6.1. Options

General

Save Tool Options On Exit

> Self explanatory

Save Tool Options Now

> Self explanatory

Reset Saved Tool Options To Default Values

> Self explanatory

Guide and Grid Snapping

Snap distance

> "Snapping" to guides, or to an image grid, means that when a tool is applied by clicking somewhere on the image display, if the clicked point is near enough to a guide or grid, it is shifted exactly onto the guide or grid. Snapping to guides can be toggled using View → Snap to Guides in the image menu; and if the grid is switched on, snapping to it can be toggled using View → Snap to Grid. This preference option determines how close a clicked point must be to a guide or grid in order to be snapped onto it, in pixels.

Scaling

Default interpolation

> When you scale something, each pixel in the result is calculated by interpolating several pixels in the source. This option determines the default interpolation method: it can always be changed, though, in the Tool Options dialog.
>
> There are four choices:
>
> None
>
> This is the fastest method, but it's quite crude: you should only consider using it if your machine is very seriously speed-impaired.
>
> Linear

This used to be the default, and is good enough for most purposes.

Cubic

This is the best choice (although it can actually look worse than Linear for some types of images), but also the slowest. Since GIMP 2.6, this method is the default.

Sinc (Lanczos3)

This method performs a high quality interpolation.

Paint Options Shared Between Tools

Brush, Pattern, Gradient

You can decide here whether changing the brush etc for one tool should cause the new item to be used for all tools, or whether each individual tool (pencil, paintbrush, airbrush, etc) should remember the item that was last used for it specifically.

Move tool

Set layer or path as active

You can decide here whether changing the current layer or path when using the move tool and without pressing any key.

1.7. Toolbox

Figure 12.7. Toolbox Preferences

1.7.1. Options

Figure 12.8. Default Toolbox appearance

This page lets you customize the appearance of the Toolbox, by deciding whether the three "context information" areas should be shown at the bottom.

Appearance

Show foreground and background color

> Controls whether the color area on the left (2) appears in the Toolbox.

Show active brush, pattern, and gradient

> Controls whether the area in the center (3), with the brush, pattern, and gradient icons, appears in the Toolbox.

Show active image

> Controls whether a preview of the currently active image appears on the right (4).

Tools configuration

In this list, tools with an eye are present in the Toolbox. By default, color tools have no eye: you can add them to the Toolbox by clicking the corresponding checkbox.

You can also sort tools by priority using the arrow up and down buttons at the bottom of the dialog.

This option replaces the Tools Dialog of former GIMP versions.

1.8. Default Image Preferences

Figure 12.9. Default New Image Preferences

This tab lets you customize the default settings for the New Image dialog. See the New Image Dialog section for an explanation of what each of the values means.

1.9. Default Image Grid

Figure 12.10. Default Grid Preferences

This page lets you customize the default properties of GIMP's grid, which can be toggled on or off using View → Show Grid from the image menu. The settings here match those in the Configure Image Grid dialog, which can be used to reconfigure the grid for an existing image, by choosing Image → Configure Grid from the image menu. See the **Configure Grid dialog** section for information on the meaning of each of the settings.

1.10. Image Windows

Figure 12.11. General Image Window Preference

This page lets you customize several aspects of the behaviour of image windows.

1.10.1. Options

General

Use "Dot for dot" by default

> Using "Dot for dot" means that at 1:1 zoom, each pixel is the image is scaled to one pixel on the display. If "Dot for dot" is not used, then the displayed image size is determined by the X and Y resolution of the image. See the **Scale Image** section for more information.

Marching ants speed

> When you create a selection, the edge of it is shown as a dashed line with dashes that appear to move, marching slowly along the boundary: they are jokingly called "marching ants". The smaller the value entered here, the faster the ants march (and consequently the more distracting they are!).

Zoom and Resize Behavior

Resize window on zoom

> If this option is checked, then each time you zoom the image, the image window will automatically resize to follow it. Otherwise, the image window will maintain the same size when you zoom the image.

Resize window on image size change

> If this option is checked, then each time change the size of the image, by cropping or resizing it, the image window will automatically resize to follow. Otherwise, the image window will maintain the same size.

Initial zoom ratio

> You can choose either to have images, when they are first opened, scaled so that the whole image fits comfortably on your display, or else shown at 1:1 zoom. If you choose the second option, and the image is too large to fit on your display, then the image window will show only part of it (but you will be able to scroll to other parts).

Space bar

While space bar is pressed

- Pan view (default) or
- Toogle to Move Tool
- No action

Mouse Cursors

Show brush outline

> If this option is checked, then when you use a paint tool, the outline of the brush will be shown on the image as you move the pointer around. On slow systems, if the brush is very large, this could occasionally cause some lag in GIMP's ability to follow your movements: if so, switching this off might help. Otherwise, you will probably find it quite useful.

Show paint tool cursor

> If this is checked, a cursor will be shown. This is in addition to the brush outline, if the brush outline is being shown. The type of cursor is determined by the next option.

Cursor mode

> This option has no effect unless Show paint tool cursor is checked. If it is, you have three choices: Tool icon, which causes a small iconic representation of the currently active tool to be shown beside the cursor; Tool icon with crosshair, which shows the icon as well as a crosshair indicating the center of the cursor; or Crosshair only.

Cursor rendering

> If you choose "Fancy" here, the cursor is drawn in grayscale. If you choose "Black and White", it is drawn in a simpler way that may speed things up a little bit if you have speed issues.

1.11. Image Window Appearance

Figure 12.12. Image Window Appearance Defaults

This page lets you customize the default appearance of image windows, for normal mode and for fullscreen mode. All of the settings here can be altered on an image-specific basis using entries in the View menu. See the **Image Window** section for information on the meaning of the entries.

The only parts that may need further explanation are the ones related to padding. "Padding" is the color shown around the edges of the image, if it does not occupy all of the display area (shown in light gray in all the figures here).

You can choose among four colors for the padding color: to use the color specified by the current theme; to use the light or dark colors specified for checks, such as represent transparent parts of the image; or to use a custom color, which can be set using the color button for "Custom padding color".

1.12. Image Window Title and Statusbar

Figure 12.13. Image Window Title and Statusbar formats

This page lets you customize the text that appears in two places: the title bar of an image, and the status bar. The title bar should appear above the image; however this depends on cooperation from the window manager, so it is not guaranteed to work in all cases. The statusbar appears underneath the image, on the right side. See the **Image Window** section for more information.

1.12.1. Choosing a Format

You can choose among several predesigned formats, or you can create one of your own, by writing a *format string* in the entry area. Here is how to understand a format string: anything you type is shown exactly as you type it, with the exception of *variables*, whose names all begin with "%". Here is a list of the variables you can use:

Variable Meaning

%f	Bare filename of the image, or "Untitled"
%F	Full path to file, or "Untitled"
%p	Image id number (this is unique)
%i	View number, if an image has more than one display
%t	Image type (RGB, grayscale, indexed)
%z	Zoom factor as a percentage
%s	Source scale factor (zoom level = %d/%s)
%d	Destination scale factor (zoom level = %d/%s)
%Dx	Expands to x if the image is dirty, nothing otherwise
%Cx	Expands to x if the image is clean, nothing otherwise
%l	The number of layers
%L	Number of layers (long form)
%m	Memory used by the image
%n	Name of the active layer/channel
%P	id of the active layer/channel
%w	Image width in pixels
%W	Image width in real-world units
%h	Image height in pixels
%H	Image height in real-world units
%u	Unit symbol (eg. px for Pixel)
%U	Unit abbreviation
%%	A literal "%" symbol

1.13. Display

Figure 12.14. Display Preferences

This page lets you customize the way transparent parts of an image are represented, and lets you recalibrate the resolution of your monitor.

1.13.1. Options

Transparency

Transparency type

> By default, GIMP indicates transparency using a checkerboard pattern with mid-tone checks, but you can change this if you want, either to a different type of checkerboard, or to solid black, white, or gray.

Check size

> Here you can alter the size of the squares in the checkerboard pattern used to indicate transparency.

Figure 12.15. The Calibration dialog

Monitor Resolution

> Monitor Resolution is the ratio of pixels, horizontally and vertically, to inches. You have three ways to proceed here:
>
> - Get Resolution from windowing system. (easiest, probably inaccurate).
> - Set Manually
> - Push the Calibrate Button.

The Calibrate Dialog

> My monitor was impressively off when I tried the Calibrate Dialog. The "Calibrate Game" is fun to play. You will need a soft ruler.

1.14. Color Management

Figure 12.16. Color Management Preferences

1.14.1. Options

This page lets you customize the GIMP color management.

Some of the options let you choose a color profile from a menu. If the desired profile is not in the menu yet, you can add it by clicking on the Select color profile from disk... item.

Tip

Files containing color profiles are easily recognizable by their .icc suffix. In addition to that they are usually stored all together in only a few places. If you are running GIMP on Mac OS X, you should try /Library/ColorSync/Profiles/ and Library/Printers/[manufacturer]/Profiles.

Mode of operation

Using this option you can decide how the GIMP color management operates. There are three modes you can choose from:

- No color management: choosing this selection shuts down the color management in GIMP completely.
- Color managed display: with this selection you can enable the GIMP color management to provide a fully corrected display of the images according to the given color profile for the display.
- Print simulation: when choosing this selection, you enable the GIMP color management not only to apply the profile for the display, but also the selected printer simulation profile. Doing so, you can preview the color results of a print with that printer.

> **Note**
>
> Please note, that the GIMP color management is used to enhance the display of images and the embedding of profiles to image files only. Especially are the options you choose in this dialog in no way used for printing from within GIMP. This is because the printing is a special task done by a more specialized printing engine that is no part of GIMP.

RGB profile

   Select the default color profile for working with RGB images.

CMYK profile

   Select the default color profile for conversion between RGB for the screen work and CMYK for printing.

Monitor profile

   This option gives you two elements for interaction:

   - You should select a display profile for this option. The selected color profile is used to display GIMP on the screen.
   - If you activate the Try to use the system monitor profile option, GIMP will use the color profile provided for the displays by the operating systems color management system.

Display rendering intent

   Rendering intents, as the one you can configure with this option, are ways of dealing with colors that are out-of- **Gamut** colors present in the source space that the destination space is incapable of producing. There are four method rendering intents to choose from:

- Perceptual
- Relative colorimetric
- Saturation
- Absolute colorimetric

A description of the individual methods can be found at Rendering Intent .

Print simulation mode

You should select a printer profile for this option. The selected color profile is used for the print simulation mode.

Softproof rendering intent

This option again provides two different elements for interaction:

- You can use the menu to select the rendering intent for the soft proof. They are the same as already described for the display rendering intent.
- If you enable the Mark out of gamut colors option, all pixels that have a color that is not printable are marked by a special color. Which color is used for this can also be chosen by you. You can do this simply by clicking on the color icon on the right besides the checkbox.

File Open behaviour

Using this menu you can determine how GIMP behaves when opening a file that contains an embedded color profile that does not match the workspace sRGB. You can choose from the following entries:

- Ask what to do: if selected, GIMP will ask every time what to do.
- Keep embedded profile: if you choose this, GIMP will keep the attached profile and not convert the image to the workspace. The image is displayed correctly anyways, because the attached profile will be applied for display.
- Convert to RGB workspace: by choosing this entry GIMP will automatically use the attached color profile to convert the image to the workspace.

Note

For more explanations:

- ICC Profiles are explained in Wikipedia [WKPD-ICC].
- See OpenICC project ([OPENICC]) where GIMP and others great names of free infography contribute to.

Many profiles to load from the web:

- ICC sRGB Workspace: ICCsRGB™ [ICCsRGB]
- Microsoft sRGB Workspace: MsRGB™ [MsRGB]
- Adobe RGB98 Workspace : Adobe RGB (1998)™ [AdobeRGB]
- ECI (European Color Initiative) Profiles: ECI™ [ECI]

1.15. Input Devices

Figure 12.17. Input devices preferences

Extended Input Devices

Configure Extended Input Devices

> This large button allows you to set the devices associated with your computer: tablet, MIDI keyboard... If you have a tablet, you will see a dialog like this:

Figure 12.18. Preferences for a tablet

Save input device settings on exit

> When you check this box, GIMP remembers the tool, color, pattern and brush you were using the last time you quitted.

Save Input Device Settings Now

> Self explanatory.

Reset Saved Input Device Settings to Default Values

> Delete your settings and restore default settings.

1.16. Input Controllers

Figure 12.19. Input controllers preferences

This dialog has two lists of additional input controllers: Available Controllers on the left, Active Controllers on the right.

A click on an item will highlight it and you can move the controller from one list to the other by clicking on the respective arrow key. When you try to move a controller from the list of active controllers to the available controllers, a dialog pops up and you will have the choice of removing the controller or just disabling it.

When you double click on a (typically active) controller or alternatively click on the Edit button at the bottom of the list, you can configure this controller in a dialog window:

Main Mouse Wheel

Figure 12.20. Main Mouse Wheel

General

> Dump events from this controller
>
> This option must be checked if you want a print on the stdout of the events generated by the enabled controllers. If you want to see those event you should start GIMP from a terminal or making it to print the stdout to file by the shell redirection. The main use of this option is for debug.
>
> Enable this controller
>
> This option must be checked if you want to add a new actions to the mouse wheel.

Mouse Wheel Events

> In this window with scroll bars you have: on the left, the possible events concerning the mouse wheel, more or less associated with control keys; on the right, the action assigned to the event when it will happen. You have also two buttons, one to Edit the selected event, the other to Cancel the action of the selected event.

Some actions are assigned to events yet. They seem to be examples, as they are not functional.

Select the action allocated to the event

After selecting an event, if you click on the Edit button, you open the following dialog:

Figure 12.21. Select Controller Event Action

If an action exists yet for this event, the window will open on this action. Else, the window will display the sections that order actions. Click on an action to select it.

Main Keyboard

You can use this dialog in the same way as that of the mouse wheel. Events are related to the arrow keys of the keyboard, combined or not with control keys.

Figure 12.22. Main Keyboard

Note

You will find an example of these notions in Creating a variable size brush .

1.17. Window Management

Figure 12.23. Window Management Preferences

This page lets you customize the way windows are handled in GIMP. You should note that GIMP does not manipulate windows directly, instead it sends requests to the window manager (i. e., to Windows if you are running in Windows; to Metacity if you are running in a standard Gnome setup in Linux; etc). Because there are many window managers, and not all of them are well behaved, it cannot be guaranteed that the functions described here will actually work as described. However, if you are using a modern, standards-compliant window manager, they ought to.

1.17.1. Options

Window Manager Hints

Window type hints for the toolbox and the docks

> The choices you make here determine how the Toolbox, and the docks that hold dialogs, will be treated. You have three possibilities for them:
>
> - If you choose Normal Window, they will be treated like any other windows.
> - If you choose Utility Window, the reduce button in the title bar is absent and the docks will remain permanently on your screen.

Figure 12.24. Utility window title bar

Normal title bar

The title bar in a utility window

- If you choose Keep above, they will be kept in front of every other window at all times.

Note that changes you make here will not take effect until the next time you start GIMP.

Focus

Activate the focused image

> Normally, when you focus an image window (usually indicated by a change in the color of the frame), it becomes the "active image" for GIMP, and therefore the target for any image-related actions you perform. Some people, though, prefer to set up their window managers such that any window entered by the pointer is automatically focused. If you do this, you may find that it is inconvenient for focused images to automatically become active, and may be happier if you uncheck this option.

Window Positions

Save window positions on exit

> If this option is checked, the next time you start GIMP, you will see the same set of dialog windows, in the same positions they occupied when you last exited.

Save Window Positions Now

> This button is only useful if "Save window positions on exit" is unchecked. It allows you to set up your windows they way you like, click the button, and then have them come up in that arrangement each time you start GIMP.

Reset Saved Window Positions to Default Values

> If you decide that you are unhappy with the arrangement of windows you have saved, and would rather go back to the default arrangement than spend time moving them around, you can do so by pressing this button.

1.18. Folders

Figure 12.25. Basic Folder Preferences

This page allows you to set the locations for two important folders used by GIMP for temporary files. The pages below it allow you to customize the locations searched for resources such as brushes etc.; see **Data Folders** for a description that applies to them. You can change the folders here by editing the entries, or by pressing the buttons on the right to bring up a file chooser window.

Folders

Temp folder

> This folder is used for temporary files: files created for temporary storage of working data, and then deleted within the same GIMP session. It does not require a lot of space or high performance. By default, a subdirectory called tmp in your personal GIMP directory is used, but if that disk is very cramped for space, or has serious performance issues, you can change it to a different directory. The directory must exist and be writable by you, or bad things will happen.

Swap folder

> This is the folder used as a "memory bank" when the total size of images and data open in GIMP exceeds the available RAM. If you work with very large images, or images with many layers, or have

many images open at once, GIMP can potentially require hundreds of megabytes of swap space, so available disk space and performance are definitely things to think about for this folder. By default, it is set to your personal GIMP directory, but if you have another disk with more free space, or substantially better performance, you may see a significant benefit from moving your swap folder there. The directory must exist and be writable by you.

1.19. Data Folders

Figure 12.26. Preferences: Brush Folders

GIMP uses several types of resources – such as brushes, patterns, gradients, etc. – for which a basic set are supplied by GIMP when it is installed, and others can be created or downloaded by the user. For each such resource type, there is a Preference page that allows you to specify the *search path*: the set of directories from which items of the type in question are automatically loaded when GIMP starts. These pages all look very much the same: the page for brushes is shown to the right as an example.

By default, the search path includes two folders: a *system* folder, where items installed along with GIMP are placed, and a *personal* folder, inside your personal GIMP directory, where items added by you should be placed. The system folder should not be marked as writable, and you should not try to alter its contents. The personal folder must be marked as writable or it is useless, because there is nothing inside it except what you put there.

You can customize the search path with the buttons at the top of the dialog.

Options

Select a Folder

> If you click on one of the folders in the list, it is selected for whatever action comes next.

Add/Replace Folder

> If you type the name of a folder in the entry space, or navigate to it using the file chooser button 🗁 on the right, and then click the left button, this will replace the selected folder with the one you have specified. If nothing in the list is selected, the folder you specify will be added to the list. If the light-symbol to the left of the text entry area is red instead of green, it means that the folder you have specified does not exist. GIMP will not create it for you, so you should do this immediately.

Move Up/Down

> If you click on the up-arrow or down-arrow buttons, the selected folder will be changed to the following or preceding one in the list. Since the folders are read in order, using those buttons change the loading precedence of the items located in those folders.

Delete Folder

> If you click the trash-can button, the selected folder will be deleted from the list. (The folder itself is not affected; it is merely removed from the search path.) Deleting the system folder is probably a bad idea, but nothing prevents you from doing it.

2. Grids and Guides

You will probably have it happen many times that you need to place something in an image very precisely, and find that it is not easy to do using a mouse. Often you can get better results by using the arrow keys on the keyboard (which move the affected object one pixel at a time, or 25 pixels if you hold down the **Shift** key), but GIMP also provides you with two other aids to make positioning easier: grids and guides.

Figure 12.27. Image used for examples below

2.1. The Image Grid

Figure 12.28. Image with default grid

Each image has a grid. It is always present, but by default it is not visible until you activate it by toggling View → Show Grid in the image menu. If you want grids to be present more often than not, you can change the default behavior by checking "Show grid" in the Image Window Appearance page of the Preferences dialog. (Note that there are separate settings for Normal Mode and Fullscreen Mode.)

The default grid appearance, set up when you install GIMP, consists of plus-shaped black crosshairs at the grid line intersections, with grid lines spaced every 10 pixels both vertically and horizontally. You can customize the default grid using the Default Image Grid page of the Preferences dialog. If you only want to change the grid appearance for the current image, you can do so by choosing Image → Configure Grid from the image menu: this brings up the Configure Grid dialog.

Figure 12.29. A different grid style

Not only can a grid be helpful for judging distances and spatial relationships, it can also permit you to align things exactly with the grid, if you toggle View → Snap to Grid in the image menu: this causes the pointer to "warp" perfectly to any grid line located within a certain distance. You can customize the snap distance threshold by setting "Snap distance" in the Tool Options page of the Preferences dialog, but most people seem to be happy with the default value of 8 pixels. (Note that it is perfectly possible to snap to the grid even if the grid is not visible. It isn't easy to imagine why you might want to do this, though.)

2.2. Guides

Figure 12.30. Image with four guides

In addition to the image grid, GIMP also gives you a more flexible type of positioning aid: *guides*. These are horizontal or vertical lines you can temporarily display on an image while you are working on it.

To create a guide, simply click on one of the rulers in the image window and pull out a guide, while holding the mouse button pressed. The guide is then displayed as a blue, dashed line, which follows the pointer. As soon as you create a guide, the "Move" tool is activated and the mouse pointer changes to the Move icon.

You can also create a guide with the New Guide command, which allows you to precisely place the guide on the image, the New Guide (by Percent) command, or the New Guides from Selection command.

You can create as many guides as you like, positioned wherever you like. To move a guide after you have created it, activate the Move tool in the Toolbox (or press the **M** key), you can then click and drag a guide. To delete a guide, simply drag it outside the image. Holding down the **Shift** key, you can move everything but a guide, using the guides as an effective alignment aid.

The behavior of the guides depends upon the Move (Affect) mode of the "Move" tool. When *Layer* mode is selected, the mouse pointer turns into a small hand as soon as it gets close to a guide. Then the guide is activated and it turns red, and you can move the guide or delete it by moving it back into the ruler. If *Selection* mode is selected, you can position a guide, but you cannot move it after that.

As with the grid, you can cause the pointer to snap to nearby guides, by toggling View → Snap to Guides in the image menu. If you have a number of guides and they are making it difficult for you to judge the image properly, you can hide them by toggling View → Show Guides. It is suggested that you only do this momentarily, otherwise you may get confused the next time you try to create a guide and don't see anything happening.

If it makes things easier for you, you can change the default behavior for guides in the Image Windows Appearance page of the Preferences dialog. Disabling Show guides is probably a bad idea, though, for the reason just given.

You can remove the guides with the Image → Guides → Remove all Guides command.

3. Rendering a Grid

How can you create a grid that is actually part of the image? You can't do this using the image grid: that is only an aid, and is only visible on the monitor or in a screenshot. You can, however, use the Grid plugin to render a grid very similar to the image grid. (Actually, the plugin has substantially more options.)

4. How to Set Your Tile Cache

During the data processing and manipulation of pictures, GIMP becomes in the need of much main memory. The more is available the better is. GIMP uses the operating system memory available resources as effectively as possible, striving to maintain the work on the pictures fast and comfortable for the user. That Data memory, during the treatment, is organized in buffered blocks of graphic data, which could exist in two different forms of data memory: in the slow not removable disk or in the fast main RAM memory. GIMP uses preferably the RAM, and when it runs short of this memory, it uses the hard disk for the remaining data. These chunks of graphic data are commonly referred to as "tiles" and the entire system is called "tile cache".

A low value for tile cache means that GIMP sends data to the disk very quickly, not making real use of the available RAM, and making the disks work for no real reason. Too high a value for tile cache, and other applications start to have less system resources, forcing them to use swap space, which also makes the disks work too hard; some of them may even terminate or start to malfunction due lack of RAM.

How do you choose a number for the Tile Cache size? Here are some tips to help you decide what value to use, as well as a few tricks:

- The easiest method is to just forget about this and hope the default works. This was a usable method when computers had little RAM, and most people just tried to make small images with GIMP while running one or two other applications at the same time. If you want something easy and only use GIMP to make screenshots and logos, this is probably the best solution.
- If you have a modern computer with plenty of memory–say, 512 MB or more–setting the Tile Cache to half of your RAM will probably give good performance for GIMP in most situations without depriving other applications. Probably even 3/4 of your RAM would be fine.
- Ask someone to do it for you, which in the case of a computer serving multiple users at the same time can be a good idea: that way the administrator and other users do not get mad at you for abusing the machine, nor do you get a badly underperforming GIMP. If it is your machine and only serves a single user at a given time, this could mean money, or drinks, as price for the service.
- Start changing the value a bit each time and check that it goes faster and faster with each increase, but the system does not complain about lack of memory. Be forewarned that sometimes lack of memory shows up suddenly with some applications being killed to make space for the others.
- Do some simple math and calculate a viable value. Maybe you will have to tune it later, but maybe you have to tune it anyway with the other previous methods. At least you know what is happening and can get the best from your computer.

Let's suppose you prefer the last option, and want to get a good value to start with. First, you need to get some data about your computer. This data is the amount of RAM installed in your system, the operating system's swap space available, and a general idea about the speed of the disks that store the operating system's swap and the directory used for GIMP's swap. You do not need to do disk tests, nor check the RPM of the disks, the thing is to see which one seems clearly faster or slower, or whether all are similar. You can change GIMP's swap directory in the Folders page of the Preferences dialog.

The next thing to do is to see how much resources you require for other apps you want to run at the same time than GIMP. So start all your tools and do some work with them, except GIMP of course, and check the usage. You can use applications like free or top, depending in what OS and what environment you use. The numbers you want is the memory left, including file cache. Modern Unix keeps a very small area free, in order to be able to keep large file and buffer caches. Linux's *free* command does the maths for you: check the column that says "free", and the line "-/+ buffers/cache". Note down also the free swap.

Now time for decisions and a bit of simple math. Basically the concept is to decide if you want to base all Tile Cache in RAM, or RAM plus operating system swap:

1. Do you change applications a lot? Or keep working in GIMP for a long time? If you spend a lot of time in GIMP, you can consider free RAM plus free swap as available; if not, you need to go to the following steps. (If you're feeling unsure about it, check the following steps.) If you are sure you switch apps every few minutes, only count the free RAM and just go to the final decision; no more things to check.
2. Does the operating system swap live in the same physical disk as GIMP swap? If so, add RAM and swap. Otherwise go to the next step.
3. Is the disk that holds the OS swap faster or the same speed as the disk that holds the GIMP swap? If slower, take only the free RAM; if faster or similar, add free RAM and swap.
4. You now have a number, be it just the free RAM or the free RAM plus the free OS swap. Reduce it a bit, to be on the safe side, and that is the Tile Cache you could use as a good start.

As you can see, all is about checking the free resources, and decide if the OS swap is worth using or will cause more problems than help.

There are some reasons you want to adjust this value, though. The basic one is changes in your computer usage pattern, or changing hardware. That could mean your assumptions about how you use your computer, or the speed of it, are no longer valid. That would require a reevaluation of the previous steps, which can drive you to a similar value or a completely new value.

Another reason to change the value is because it seems that GIMP runs too slowly, while changing to other applications is fast: this means that GIMP could use more memory without impairing the other applications. On the other hand, if you get complaints from other applications about not having enough memory, then it may benefit you to not let GIMP hog so much of it.

If you decided to use only RAM and GIMP runs slowly, you could try increasing the value a bit, but never to use also all the free swap. If the case is the contrary, using both RAM and swap, and you have problems about lack of resources, then you should decrease the amount of RAM available to GIMP.

Another trick is to put the Swap Dir on a very fast disk, or on a different disk than the one where most of your files reside. Spreading the operating system swap file over multiple disks is also a good way to speed things up, in general. And of course, you might have to buy more RAM or stop using lots of programs at the same time: you can not expect to edit a poster on a computer with 16MB and be fast.

You can also check what memory requirements your images have. The larger the images, and the number of undoes, the more resources you need. This is another way to choose a number, but it is only good if you always work with the same kind of images, and thus the real requirements do not vary. It is also helpful to know if you will require more RAM and/or disk space.

5. Creating Shortcuts to Menu Functions

Many functions which are accessible via the image menu have a default keyboard shortcut. You may want to create a new shortcut for a command that you use a lot and doesn't have one or, more rarely, edit an existing shortcut. There are two methods for doing this.

Procedure 12.1. Using dynamic keyboard shortcuts

1. First, you have to activate this capability by checking the Use dynamic keyboard shortcuts option in the Interface item of the Preferences menu. This option is usually not checked, to prevent accidental key presses from creating an unwanted shortcut.
2. While you're doing that, also check the Save keyboard shortcuts on exit option so that your shortcut will be saved.
3. To create a keyboard shortcut, simply place the mouse pointer on a command in the menu: it will then be highlighted. Be careful that the mouse pointer doesn't move and type a sequence of three keys, keeping the keys pressed. You will see this sequence appear on the right of the command.

4. It is best to use the **Ctrl+Alt+Key** sequence for your custom shortcuts.

Figure 12.31. Configure Keyboard Shortcuts

Procedure 12.2. Using the Keyboard Shortcut Editor

1. You get to this Editor by clicking on Configure keyboard shortcuts in the "Interface" item of the Preferences menu.
2. As shown in this dialog, you can select the command you want to create a shortcut for, in the "Action" area. Then you type your key sequence as above. In principle, the Space bar should clear a shortcut. (In practice, it clears it, but doesn't delete it.)
3. This shortcut editor also allows you to *control the tool parameter settings* with the keyboard. At the top of this dialog, you can find a Context menu that takes you to the tool parameters. To make your work easier, tool types are marked with small icons.

Note

Custom Keyboard shortcuts are stored in one of Gimp's hidden directory (/home/[username]/.gimp-2.8/menurc) under Linux, and C:\Documents and Settings\[Username]\.gimp-2.8\menurc under Windows XP. It is a simple text file that you can transport from one computer to another.

6. Customize Splash-Screen

When you start GIMP, you see the *splash-screen* displaying short status messages while the program is loading all its components.

Of course, you can customize the splash-screen: Create a splashes directory in your in your personal GIMP folder (/home/user_name/.gimp-2.8 on Linux, C:\Documents and Settings\user_name\.gimp-2.8\ on Windows).

Copy your image(s) into this splashes directory. On start, GIMP will read this directory and choose one of the images at random.

Tip

Make sure that your images aren't too small.

Chapter 13. Scripting
1. Plugins
1.1. Introduction

One of the nicest things about GIMP is how easily its functionality can be extended, by using plugins. GIMP plugins are external programs that run under the control of the main GIMP application and interact with it very closely. Plugins can manipulate images in almost any way that users can. Their advantage is that it is much easier to add a capability to GIMP by writing a small plugin than by modifying the huge mass of complex code that makes up the GIMP core. Many valuable plugins have C source code that only comes to 100-200 lines or so.

Several dozen plugins are included in the main GIMP distribution, and installed automatically along with GIMP. Most of them can be accessed through the Filters menu (in fact, everything in that menu is a plugin), but a number are located in other menus. In many cases you can use one without ever realizing that it is a plugin: for example, the "Normalize" function for automatic color correction is actually a plugin, although there is nothing about the way it works that would tell you this.

In addition to the plugins included with GIMP , many more are available on the net. A large number can be found at the GIMP Plugin Registry GIMP-REGISTRY, a web site whose purpose is to provide a central repository for plugins. Creators of plugins can upload them there; users in search of plugins for a specific purpose can search the site in a variety of ways.

Anybody in the world can write a GIMP plugin and make it available over the web, either via the Registry or a personal web site, and many very valuable plugins can be obtained in this way some are described elsewhere in the User's Manual. With this freedom from constraint comes a certain degree of risk, though: the fact that anybody can do it means that there is no effective quality control. The plugins distributed with GIMP have all been tested and tuned by the developers, but many that you can download were just hacked together in a few hours and then tossed to the winds. Some plugin creators just don't care about robustness, and even for those who do, their ability to test on a variety of systems in a variety of situations is often quite limited. Basically, when you download a plugin, you are getting something for free, and sometimes you get exactly what you pay for. This is not said in an attempt to discourage you, just to make sure you understand reality.

Warning

Plugins, being full-fledged executable programs, can do any of the things that any other program can do, including install back-doors on your system or otherwise compromise its security. Don't install a plugin unless it comes from a trusted source.

These caveats apply as much to the Plugin Registry as to any other source of plugins. The Registry is available to any plugin creator who wants to use it: there is no systematic oversight. Obviously if the maintainers became aware that something evil was there, they would remove it. (That hasn't happened yet.) There is, however, for GIMP and its plugins the same warranty as for any other free software: namely, none.

Caution

Plugins have been a feature of GIMP for many versions. However, plugins written for one version of GIMP can hardly ever be used successfully with other versions. They need to be ported: sometimes this is easy, sometimes not. Many plugins are already available in several versions. Bottom line: before trying to install a plugin, make sure that it is written for your version of GIMP.

1.2. Using Plugins

For the most part you can use a plugin like any other GIMP tool, without needing to be aware that it is a plugin. But there are a few things about plugins that are useful to understand.

One is that plugins are generally not as robust as the GIMP core. When GIMP crashes, it is considered a very serious thing: it can cost the user a lot of trouble and headache. When a plugin crashes, the consequences are usually not so serious. In most cases you can just continuing working without worrying about it.

Note

Because plugins are separate programs, they communicate with the GIMP core in a special way: The GIMP developers call it "talking over a wire". When a plugin crashes, the communication breaks down, and you will see an error message about a "wire read error".

Tip

When a plugin crashes, GIMP gives you a very ominous-looking message telling you that the plugin may have left GIMP in a corrupted state, and you should consider saving your images and exiting. Strictly speaking, this is quite correct, because plugins have the power to alter almost anything in GIMP, but for practical purposes, experience has shown that corruption is actually quite rare, and many users just continue working and don't worry about it. Our advice is that you simply think about how much trouble it would cause you if something went wrong, and weigh it against the odds.

Because of the way plugins communicate with GIMP, they do not have any mechanism for being informed about changes you make to an image after the plugin has been started. If you start a plugin, and then alter the image using some other tool, the plugin will often crash, and when it doesn't will usually give a bogus result. You should avoid running more than one plugin at a time on an image, and avoid doing anything to the image until the plugin has finished working on it. If you ignore this advice, not only will you probably screw up the image, you will probably screw up the undo system as well, so that you won't even be able to recover from your foolishness.

1.3. Installing New Plugins

The plugins that are distributed with GIMP don't require any special installation. Plugins that you download yourself do. There are several scenarios, depending on what OS you are using and how the plugin is structured. In Linux it is usually pretty easy to install a new plugin; in Windows, it is either easy or very hard. In any case, the two are best considered separately.

1.3.1. Linux / Unix-sytem like systems

Most plugins fall into two categories: small ones whose source code is distributed as a single .c file, and larger ones whose source code is distributed as a directory containing multiple files including a Makefile.

For a simple one-file plugin, call it borker.c, installing it is just a matter of running the command **gimptool-2.0 --install borker.c**. This command compiles the plugin and installs it in your personal plugin directory, ~/gimp-2.4/plugins unless you have changed it. This will cause it to be loaded automatically the next time you start GIMP. You don't need to be root to do these things; in fact, you shouldn't be. If the plugin fails to compile, well, be creative.

Once you have installed the plugin, how do you activate it? The menu path is determined by the plugin itself, so to answer this you need to either look at the documentation for the plugin (if there is any), or launch the Plugin Description dialog (from Xtns/Plugins Details) search the plug-in by its name and look of the Tree view tab. If you still don't find, finally explore the menus or look at the source code in the Register section -- whichever is easiest.

For more complex plugins, organized as a directory with multiple files, there ought to be a file inside called either INSTALL or README, with instructions.

If not, the best advice is to toss the plugin in the trash and spend your time on something else: any code written with so little concern for the user is likely to be frustrating in myriad ways.

Some plugins (specifically those based on the GIMP Plugin Template) are designed to be installed in the main system GIMP directory, rather than your home directory. For these, you will need to be root to perform the final stage of installation (when issuing the **make install** command).

If you install in your personal plugin directory a plugin that has the same name as one in the system plugin directory, only one can be loaded, and it will be the one in your home directory. You will receive messages telling you this each time you start GIMP. This is probably a situation best avoided.

1.3.2. Windows

Windows is a much more problematic environment for building software than Linux. Every decent Linux distribution comes fully supplied with tools for compiling software, and they are all very similar in the way they work, but Windows does not come with such tools. It is possible to set up a good software-building environment in Windows, but it requires either a substantial amount of money or a substantial amount of effort and knowledge.

What this means in relation to GIMP plugins is the following: either you have an environment in which you can build software, or you don't. If you don't, then your best hope is to find a precompiled version of the plugin somewhere (or persuade somebody to compile it for you), in which case you simply need to put it into your personal plugin directory. If you do have an environment in which you can build software (which for present purposes means an environment in which you can build GIMP), then you no doubt already know quite a bit about these things, and just need to follow the Linux instructions.

1.3.3. Apple Mac OS X

How you install plugins on OS X mostly depends on how you installed GIMP itself. If you were one of the brave and installed GIMP through one of the package managers like fink [DARWINORTS] or darwinports, [FINK] the plugin installation works exactly the way it is described for the Linux platform already. The only difference is, that a couple of plugins might be even available in the repository of you package manager, so give it a try.

If you on the other hand are one of the Users that preferred to grab a prebuild GIMP package like GIMP.app, you most probably want to stick to that prebuild stuff. So you can try to get a prebuild version of the plugin of you dreams from the author of the plugin, but I'd not want to bet on this. Building your own binaries unfortunately involves installing GIMP through one of the package managers mentioned above.

1.4. Writing Plugins

If you want to learn how to write a plugin, you can find plenty of help at the GIMP Developers web site [GIMP-DEV-PLUGIN]. GIMP is a complex program, but the development team has made strenuous efforts to flatten the learning curve for plugin writing: there are good instructions and examples, and the main library that plugins use to interface with GIMP (called "libgimp") has a well-documented API. Good programmers, learning by modifying existing plugins, are often able to accomplish interesting things after just a couple of days of work.

2. Using Script-Fu Scripts

2.1. Script-Fu?

Script-Fu is what the Windows world would call "macros" But Script-Fu is more powerful than that. Script-Fu is based on an interpreting language called Scheme, and works by using querying functions to the GIMP database. You can do all kinds of things with Script-Fu, but an ordinary GIMP user will probably use it for automating things that:

- You want to do frequently.
- Are really complicated to do, and hard to remember.

Remember that you can do a whole lot with Script-Fu. The scripts that come with GIMP can be quite useful, but they can also serve as models for learning Script-Fu, or at least as a framework and source of modification when you make your own script. Read the Script-Fu Tutorial in the next section if you want to learn more about how to make scripts.

We will describe some of the most useful scripts in this chapter, but we won't cover them all. There are simply too many scripts. Some of the scripts are also very simple and you will probably not need any documentation to be able to use them.

Script-Fu (a dialect of Scheme) isn't the only scripting language available for GIMP. But Script-Fu is the only scripting language that is installed by default. Other available scripting extensions are Perl and Tcl. You can download and install both extensions at the GIMP Plugin Registry [GIMP-REGISTRY].

2.2. Installing Script-Fus

One of the great things about Script-Fu is that you can share your script with all your GIMP friends. There are many scripts that come with GIMP by default, but there are also vast quantities of scripts that are available for download all around the Internet.

1. If you have downloaded a script, copy or move it to your scripts directory. It can be found in the Preferences: Folders → Scripts.
2. Do a refresh by using Filters → Script-Fu → Refresh Scripts from the image menubar. The script will now appear in one of your menus. If you don't find it, look for it under the root file menu filters. If it doesn't appear at all, something was wrong with the script (e.g. it contains syntax errors).

2.3. Do's and Don'ts

A common error when you are dealing with Script-Fus is that you simply bring them up and press the OK button. When nothing happens, you probably think that the script is broken or buggy, but there is most likely nothing wrong with it.

2.4. Different Kinds Of Script-Fus

There are two kinds of Script-Fus:

Standalone Script-Fus

> You will find the standalone variants under File → Create → Type of Script in the image menubar (see the figure below).

Figure 13.1. Script-Fus by category

Image-dependent Script-Fus

Menus have been reorganized. A new Colors-menu appears. It groups together all scripts that work on colors, for example tools that adjust hue, saturation, lightness..., filters...etc. Filters-menu and Script-Fu-menu are merged in one Filters-menu and it is organized according to new categories. Image-dependent Plug-ins and Script-Fus are now disseminated in the image-menus. For example, Color to Alpha filter is in Colors-menu. At the beginning, it's disconcerting, but you finish to get used to this because it's more logical.

The figure below show where you can find them in the image-menu.

Figure 13.2. Where find Image-dependent scripts

2.5. Standalone Scripts

We will not try to describe every script in depth. Most Script-Fus are very easy to understand and use. At the time of this writing, the following types are installed by default:

- Patterns
- Web page themes
- Logos
- Buttons

Patterns

> You will find all kinds of pattern-generating scripts here. Generally, they are quite useful because you can add many arguments to your own patterns.
>
> We'll take a look at the Land script. In this script you have to set the image/pattern size, and specify what levels of random to use for your land creation. The colors used to generate the land map are taken from the currently selected gradient in the gradient editor. You must also supply values for the level of detail, land and sea height/depth and the

scale. Scale refers to the scale of your map, just as in an ordinary road map, 1:10 will be typed as 10.

Web Page Themes

Here is clearly a practical use for scripts. By creating a script for making custom text, logos, buttons arrows, etc., for your web site, you will give them all the same style and shape. You will also be saving a lot of time, because you don't have to create every logo, text or button by hand.

Most of the scripts are quite self-explanatory, but here are some hints:

- Leave all strange characters like ' and " intact.
- Make sure that the pattern specified in the script exists.
- Padding refers to the amount of space around your text.
- A high value for bevel width gives the illusion of a higher button.
- If you type TRUE for "Press", the button will look pushed down.
- Choose transparency if you don't want a solid background. If you choose a solid background, make sure it is the same color as the web page background.

Logos

Here you will find all kinds of logo-generating scripts. This is nice, but use it with care, as people might recognize your logo as being made by a known GIMP script. You should rather regard it as a base that you can modify to fit your needs. The dialog for making a logo is more or less the same for all such scripts:

1. In the Text String field, type your logo name, like Frozenriver.
2. In the Font Size text field, type the size of your logo in pixels.
3. In the Font text field, type the name of the font that you want to use for your logo.
4. To choose the color of your logo, just click on the color button. This brings up a color dialog.
5. If you look at the current command field, you can watch the script run.

Make Buttons

Under this headline you'll find two scripts that makes rectangular beveled buttons, with or without round corners (Round Button or Simple Beveled Button). They have a dozen parameters or so, and most of them are similar to those in the logo scripts. You can experiment with different settings to come up with a button you like.

2.6. Image-Dependent Scripts

Now, scripts and filters that perform operations on an existing image are accessible directly by the appropriate menu. For example, the script New Brush (script-fu-paste-as-brush) is integrated in the Edit image menu (Edit → Paste as... → New Brush), that is more logical.

Furthermore, a new Color menu has been created that regroups together all that concern works on colors, the hue or level color adjustment tools, etc...

Filters menu and Scripts-Fu menu are regrouped in one Filters menu and organised according to new categories. Now if a plugin and a filter works similarly, they are nearby in the menu.

The Scripts-Fu menu only appears if you have loaded additional scripts: for example the gimp-resynthesizer pack corresponding to your Linux distribution (.deb, .rpm, .gz ...).

3. A Script-Fu Tutorial

In this training course, we'll introduce you to the fundamentals of Scheme necessary to use Script-Fu, and then build a handy script that you can add to your toolbox of scripts. The script prompts the user for some text, then creates a new image sized perfectly to the text. We will then enhance the script to allow for a buffer of space around the text. We will conclude with a few suggestions for ways to ramp up your knowledge of Script-Fu.

> **Note**
> This section as adapted from a tutorial written for the GIMP 1 User Manual by Mike Terry.

3.1. Getting Acquainted With Scheme
3.1.1. Let's Start Scheme'ing

The first thing to learn is that:

Every statement in Scheme is surrounded by parentheses ().

The second thing you need to know is that:

The function name/operator is always the first item in the parentheses, and the rest of the items are parameters to the function.

However, not everything enclosed in parentheses is a function — they can also be items in a list — but we'll get to that later. This notation is referred to as prefix notation, because the function prefixes everything else. If you're familiar with postfix notation, or own a calculator that uses Reverse Polish Notation (such as most HP calculators), you should have no problem adapting to formulating expressions in Scheme.

The third thing to understand is that:

Mathematical operators are also considered functions, and thus are listed first when writing mathematical expressions.

This follows logically from the prefix notation that we just mentioned.

3.1.2. Examples Of Prefix, Infix, And Postfix Notations

Here are some quick examples illustrating the differences between *prefix*, *infix*, and *postfix* notations. We'll add a 1 and 23 together:

- Prefix notation: **+ 1 23** (the way Scheme will want it)
- Infix notation: **1 + 23** (the way we "normally" write it)
- Postfix notation: **1 23 +** (the way many HP calculators will want it)

3.1.3. Practicing In Scheme

Now, let's practice what we have just learned. Start up GIMP, if you have not already done so, and choose Filters → Script-Fu → Console. This will start up the Script-Fu Console window, which allows us to work interactively in Scheme. In a matter of moments, the Script-Fu Console will appear:

3.1.4. The Script-Fu Console Window

At the bottom of this window is an entry-field ought to be entitled Current Command. Here, we can test out simple Scheme commands interactively. Let's start out easy, and add some numbers:

(+ 3 5)

Typing this in and hitting **Enter** yields the expected answer of 8 in the center window.

Figure 13.3. Use Script-Fu Console.

Now, what if we wanted to add more than one number? The "+" function can take two or more arguments, so this is not a problem:

(+ 3 5 6)

This also yields the expected answer of 14.

So far, so good — we type in a Scheme statement and it's executed immediately in the Script-Fu Console window. Now for a word of caution...

3.1.5. Watch Out For Extra Parentheses

If you're like me, you're used to being able to use extra parentheses whenever you want to — like when you're typing a complex mathematical equation and you want to separate the parts by parentheses to make it clearer when you read it. In Scheme, you have to be careful and not insert these extra parentheses incorrectly. For example, say we wanted to add 3 to the result of adding 5 and 6 together:

3 + (5 + 6) + 7 = ?

Knowing that the + operator can take a list of numbers to add, you might be tempted to convert the above to the following:

(+ 3 (5 6) 7)

However, this is incorrect — remember, every statement in Scheme starts and ends with parens, so the Scheme interpreter will think that you're trying to call a function named "5" in the second group of parens, rather than summing those numbers before adding them to 3.

The correct way to write the above statement would be:

(+ 3 (+ 5 6) 7)

3.1.6. Make Sure You Have The Proper Spacing, Too

If you are familiar with other programming languages, like C/C++, Perl or Java, you know that you don't need white space around mathematical operators to properly form an expression:

    3+5, 3 +5, 3+ 5

These are all accepted by C/C++, Perl and Java compilers. However, the same is not true for Scheme. You must have a space after a mathematical operator (or any other function name or operator) in Scheme for it to be correctly interpreted by the Scheme interpreter.

Practice a bit with simple mathematical equations in the Script-Fu Console until you're totally comfortable with these initial concepts.

3.2. Variables And Functions

Now that we know that every Scheme statement is enclosed in parentheses, and that the function name/operator is listed first, we need to know how to create and use variables, and how to create and use functions. We'll start with the variables.

3.2.1. Declaring Variables

Although there are a couple of different methods for declaring variables, the preferred method is to use the **let*** construct. If you're familiar with other programming languages, this construct is equivalent to defining a list of local variables and a scope in which they're active. As an example, to declare two variables, a and b, initialized to 1 and 2, respectively, you'd write:

```
(let*
  (
    (a 1)
```

```
      (b 2)
    )
    (+ a b)
)
```

or, as one line:

(let* ((a 1) (b 2)) (+ a b))

> **Note**
>
> You'll have to put all of this on one line if you're using the console window. In general, however, you'll want to adopt a similar practice of indentation to help make your scripts more readable. We'll talk a bit more about this in the section on White Space.

This declares two local variables, a and b, initializes them, then prints the sum of the two variables.

3.2.2. What Is A Local Variable?

You'll notice that we wrote the summation (+ a b) within the parens of the let* expression, not after it.

This is because the let* statement defines an area in your script in which the declared variables are usable; if you type the (+ a b) statement after the (let* ...) statement, you'll get an error, because the declared variables are only valid within the context of the let* statement; they are what programmers call local variables.

3.2.3. The General Syntax Of let*

The general form of a let* statement is:

(let* (*variables*)
  expressions)

where variables are declared within parens, e.g., (a 2), and expressions are any valid Scheme expressions. Remember that the variables declared here are only valid within the let* statement — they're local variables.

3.2.4. White Space

Previously, we mentioned the fact that you'll probably want to use indentation to help clarify and organize your scripts. This is a good policy to adopt, and is not a problem in Scheme — white space is ignored by the Scheme interpreter, and can thus be liberally applied to help clarify and organize the code within a script. However, if you're working in Script-Fu's Console window, you'll have to enter an entire expression on one line; that is, everything between the opening and closing parens of an expression must come on one line in the Script-Fu Console window.

3.2.5. Assigning A New Value To A Variable

Once you've initialized a variable, you might need to change its value later on in the script. Use the set! statement to change the variable's value:

```
(let* ( (theNum 10) ) (set! theNum (+ theNum theNum)) )
```

Try to guess what the above statement will do, then go ahead and enter it in the Script-Fu Console window.

Note

The "\" indicates that there is no line break. Ignore it (don't type it in your Script-Fu console and don't hit **Enter**), just continue with the next line.

3.2.6. Functions

Now that you've got the hang of variables, let's get to work with some functions. You declare a function with the following syntax:

```
(define
  (
    name
    param-list
  )
  expressions
)
```

where *name* is the name assigned to this function, *param-list* is a space-delimited list of parameter names, and *expressions* is a series of expressions that the function executes when it's called. For example:

```
(define (AddXY inX inY) (+ inX inY) )
```

AddXY is the function's name and inX and inY are the variables. This function takes its two parameters and adds them together.

If you've programmed in other imperative languages (like C/C++, Java, Pascal, etc.), you might notice that a couple of things are absent in this function definition when compared to other programming languages.

- First, notice that the parameters don't have any "types" (that is, we didn't declare them as strings, or integers, etc.). Scheme is a type-less language. This is handy and allows for quicker script writing.
- Second, notice that we don't need to worry about how to "return" the result of our function — the last statement is the value "returned" when calling this function. Type the function into the console, then try something like:

(AddXY (AddXY 5 6) 4)

3.3. Lists, Lists And More Lists

We've trained you in variables and functions, and now enter the murky swamps of Scheme's lists.

3.3.1. Defining A List

Before we talk more about lists, it is necessary that you know the difference between atomic values and lists.

You've already seen atomic values when we initialized variables in the previous lesson. An atomic value is a single value. So, for example, we can assign the variable "x" the single value of 8 in the following statement:

(let* ((x 8)) x)

(We added the expression x at the end to print out the value assigned to x— normally you won't need to do this. Notice how let* operates just like a function: The value of the last statement is the value returned.)

A variable may also refer to a list of values, rather than a single value. To assign the variable x the list of values 1, 3, 5, we'd type:

(let* ((x '(1 3 5))) x)

Try typing both statements into the Script-Fu Console and notice how it replies. When you type the first statement in, it simply replies with the result:

8

However, when you type in the other statement, it replies with the following result:

(1 3 5)

When it replies with the value 8 it is informing you that x contains the atomic value 8. However, when it replies with (1 3 5), it is then informing you that x contains not a single value, but a list of values. Notice that there are no commas in our declaration or assignment of the list, nor in the printed result.

The syntax to define a list is:

'(a b c)

where a, b, and c are literals. We use the apostrophe (') to indicate that what follows in the parentheses is a list of literal values, rather than a function or expression.

An empty list can be defined as such:'() or simply: ()

Lists can contain atomic values, as well as other lists:

```
(let*
   (
     (x
       '("GIMP" (1 2 3) ("is" ("great" () ) ) )
     )
   )
   x
)
```

Notice that after the first apostrophe, you no longer need to use an apostrophe when defining the inner lists. Go ahead and copy the statement into the Script-Fu Console and see what it returns.

You should notice that the result returned is not a list of single, atomic values; rather, it is a list of a literal ("The GIMP"), the list (1 2 3), etc.

3.3.2. How To Think Of Lists

It's useful to think of lists as composed of a "head" and a "tail". The head is the first element of the list, the tail the rest of the list. You'll see why this is important when we discuss how to add to lists and how to access elements in the list.

3.3.3. Creating Lists Through Concatenation (The Cons Function)

One of the more common functions you'll encounter is the cons function. It takes a value and places it to its second argument, a list. From the previous section, I suggested that you think of a list as being composed of an element (the head) and the remainder of the list (the tail). This is exactly how cons functions — it adds an element to the head of a list. Thus, you could create a list as follows:

(cons 1 '(2 3 4))

The result is the list (1 2 3 4).

You could also create a list with one element:

(cons 1 ())

You can use previously declared variables in place of any literals, as you would expect.

3.3.4. Defining A List Using The list Function

To define a list composed of literals or previously declared variables, use the list function:

(list 5 4 3 a b c)

This will compose and return a list containing the values held by the variables a, b and c. For example:

```
(let* (
    (a 1)
    (b 2)
    (c 3)
)
    (list 5 4 3 a b c)
)
```

This code creates the list (5 4 3 1 2 3).

3.3.5. Accessing Values In A List

To access the values in a list, use the functions car and cdr, which return the first element of the list and the rest of the list, respectively. These functions break the list down into the head::tail construct I mentioned earlier.

3.3.6. The car Function

car returns the first element of the list (the head of the list). The list needs to be non-null. Thus, the following returns the first element of the list:

(car '("first" 2 "third"))

which is:

"first"

3.3.7. The *cdr* function

cdr returns the rest of the list after the first element (the tail of the list). If there is only one element in the list, it returns an empty list.

(cdr '("first" 2 "third"))

returns:

(2 "third")

whereas the following:

(cdr '("one and only"))

returns:

()

3.3.8. Accessing Other Elements In A List

OK, great, we can get the first element in a list, as well as the rest of the list, but how do we access the second, third or other elements of a list? There exist several "convenience" functions to access, for example, the head of the head of the tail of a list (caadr), the tail of the tail of a list (cddr), etc.

The basic naming convention is easy: The a's and d's represent the heads and tails of lists, so

(car (cdr (car x)))

could be written as:

(cadar x)

To get some practice with list-accessing functions, try typing in the following (except all on one line if you're using the console); use different variations of car and cdr to access the different elements of the list:

```
(let* (
    (x '( (1 2 (3 4 5) 6) 7 8 (9 10) )
    )
  )
  ; place your car/cdr code here
)
```

Try accessing the number 3 in the list using only two function calls. If you can do that, you're on your way to becoming a Script-Fu Master!

> **Note**
>
> In Scheme, a semicolon (;) marks a comment. It, and anything that follows it on the same line, are ignored by the script interpreter, so you can use this to add comments to jog your memory when you look at the script later.

3.4. Your First Script-Fu Script

Do you not need to stop and catch your breath? No? Well then, let's proceed with your fourth lesson — your first Script-Fu Script.

3.4.1. Creating A Text Box Script

One of the most common operations I perform in GIMP is creating a box with some text in it for a web page, a logo or whatever. However, you never quite know how big to make the initial image when you start out. You don't know how much space the text will fill with the font and font size you want.

The Script-Fu Master (and student) will quickly realize that this problem can easily be solved and automated with Script-Fu.

We will, therefore, create a script, called Text Box, which creates an image correctly sized to fit snugly around a line of text the user inputs. We'll also let the user choose the font, font size and text color.

3.4.2. Editing And Storing Your Scripts

Up until now, we've been working in the Script-Fu Console. Now, however, we're going to switch to editing script text files.

Where you place your scripts is a matter of preference — if you have access to GIMP's default script directory, you can place your scripts there. However, I prefer keeping my personal scripts in my own script directory, to keep them separate from the factory-installed scripts.

In the .gimp-2.8 directory that GIMP made off of your home directory, you should find a directory called scripts. GIMP will automatically look in your .gimp-2.8 directory for a scripts directory, and add the scripts in this directory to the Script-Fu database. You should place your personal scripts here.

3.4.3. The Bare Essentials

Every Script-Fu script defines at least one function, which is the script's main function. This is where you do the work.

Every script must also register with the procedural database, so you can access it within GIMP.

We'll define the main function first:

```
(define (script-fu-text-box inText inFont inFontSize inTextColor))
```

Here, we've defined a new function called script-fu-text-box that takes four parameters, which will later correspond to some text, a font, the font size, and the text's color. The function is currently empty and thus does nothing. So far, so good — nothing new, nothing fancy.

3.4.4. Naming Conventions

Scheme's naming conventions seem to prefer lowercase letters with hyphens, which I've followed in the naming of the function. However, I've departed from the convention with the parameters. I like more descriptive names for my parameters and variables, and thus add the "in" prefix to the parameters so I can quickly see that they're values passed into the script, rather than created within it. I use the prefix "the" for variables defined within the script.

It's GIMP convention to name your script functions script-fu-abc, because then when they're listed in the procedural database, they'll all show up under script-fu when you're listing the functions. This also helps distinguish them from plug-ins.

3.4.5. Registering The Function

Now, let's register the function with GIMP. This is done by calling the function script-fu-register. When GIMP reads in a script, it will execute this function, which registers the script with the procedural database. You can place this function call wherever you wish in your script, but I usually place it at the end, after all my other code.

Here's the listing for registering this function (I will explain all its parameters in a minute):

```
(script-fu-register
  "script-fu-text-box"              ;func name
  "Text Box"                        ;menu label
  "Creates a simple text box, sized to fit\
```

```
      around the user's choice of text,\
    font, font size, and color."        ;description
  "Michael Terry"                       ;author
  "copyright 1997, Michael Terry;\
    2009, the GIMP Documentation Team"  ;copyright notice
  "October 27, 1997"                    ;date created
  ""                 ;image type that the script works on
  SF-STRING     "Text"        "Text Box"  ;a string variable
  SF-FONT       "Font"        "Charter"   ;a font variable
  SF-ADJUSTMENT "Font size"   '(50 1 1000 1 10 0 1)
                                          ;a spin-button
  SF-COLOR      "Color"       '(0 0 0)    ;color variable
)
(script-fu-menu-register "script-fu-text-box" "<Image>/File/Create/Text")
```

If you save these functions in a text file with a .scm suffix in your script directory, then choose Filters → Script-Fu → Refresh Scripts, this new script will appear as File → Create → Text → Text Box.

If you invoke this new script, it won't do anything, of course, but you can view the prompts you created when registering the script (more information about what we did is covered next).

Finally, if you invoke the Procedure Browser (Help → Procedure Browser), you'll notice that our script now appears in the database.

3.4.6. Steps For Registering The Script

To register our script with GIMP, we call the function script-fu-register, fill in the seven required parameters and add our script's own parameters, along with a description and default value for each parameter.

The Required Parameters

- The *name* of the function we defined. This is the function called when our script is invoked (the entry-point into our script). This is necessary because we may define additional functions within the same file, and GIMP needs to know which of these functions to call. In our example, we only defined one function, text-box, which we registered.
- The *location* in the menu where the script will be inserted. The exact location of the script is specified like a path in Unix, with the root of the path being image menu as <Image>.[6]

    If your script does not operate on an existing image (and thus creates a new image, like our Text Box script will), you'll want to insert it in the image window menu, which you can access through the image menu bar, by right-clicking the image window, by clicking the menu button icon at the left-top corner of the image window, or by pressing **F10**.

If your script is intended to work on an image being edited, you'll want to insert it in the image window menu. The rest of the path points to the menu lists, menus and sub-menus. Thus, we registered our Text Box script in the Text menu of the Create menu of the File menu.[7] (File → Create → Text → Text Box).

If you notice, the Text sub-menu in the File/Create menu wasn't there when we began — GIMP automatically creates any menus not already existing.

- A *description* of your script, to be displayed in the Procedure Browser.
- *Your name* (the author of the script).
- *Copyright* information.
- The *date* the script was made, or the last revision of the script.
- The *types* of images the script works on. This may be any of the following: RGB, RGBA, GRAY, GRAYA, INDEXED, INDEXEDA. Or it may be none at all — in our case, we're creating an image, and thus don't need to define the type of image on which we work.

Figure 13.4. The menu of our script.

3.4.7. Registering The Script's Parameters

Once we have listed the required parameters, we then need to list the parameters that correspond to the parameters our script needs. When we list these params, we give hints as to what their types are. This is for the dialog which pops up when the user selects our script. We also provide a default value.

This section of the registration process has the following format:

Param Type	Description	Example
SF-IMAGE	If your script operates on an open image, this should be the first parameter after the required parameters. GIMP will pass in a reference to the image in this parameter.	3
SF-DRAWABLE	If your script operates on an open image, this should be the second parameter after the SF-IMAGE param. It refers to the active layer. GIMP will pass in a reference to the active layer in this parameter.	17
SF-VALUE	Accepts numbers and strings. Note that quotes must be escaped for default text, so better use SF-STRING.	42
SF-STRING	Accepts strings.	"Some text"
SF-COLOR	Indicates that a color is requested in this parameter.	'(0 102 255)
SF-TOGGLE	A checkbox is displayed, to get a Boolean value.	TRUE or FALSE

3.4.8. *The Script-Fu parameter API[8]*

Note

Beside the above parameter types there are more types for the interactive mode, each of them will create a widget in the control dialog. You will find a list of these parameters with descriptions and examples in the test script plug-ins/script-fu/scripts/test-sphere.scm shipped with the GIMP source code.

Param Type	Description
SF-ADJUSTMENT	Creates an adjustment widget in the dialog. SF-ADJUSTMENT "label" '(value lower upper step_inc page_inc digits type) **Widget arguments list** **Element** **Description** "label" Text printed before the widget.

	value	Value print at the start.
	lower upper	/ The lower / upper values (range of choice).
	step_inc	Increment/decrement value.
	page_inc	Increment/decrement value using page key.
	digits	Digits after the point (decimal part).
	Type	One of: SF-SLIDER or 0, SF-SPINNER or 1
SF-COLOR	Creates a color button in the dialog. SF-COLOR "label" '(red green blue) or SF-COLOR "label" "color" **Widget arguments list** **Element** **Description** "label" Text printed before the widget. '(red green blue) List of three values for the red, green and blue components. "color" Color name in CSS notatation.	
SF-FONT	Creates a font-selection widget in the dialog. It returns a fontname as a string. There are two new gimp-text procedures to ease the use of this return parameter: (gimp-text-fontname image drawable x-pos y-pos text border antialias size unit font) (gimp-text-get-extents-fontname text size unit font) where font is the fontname you get. The size specified in the fontname is silently ignored. It is	

	only used in the font-selector. So you are asked to set it to a useful value (24 pixels is a good choice). SF-FONT "label" "fontname" **Widget arguments list** **Element Description** "label" Text printed before the widget. "fontname" Name of the default font.
SF-BRUSH	It will create a widget in the control dialog. The widget consists of a preview area (which when pressed will produce a popup preview) and a button with the "..." label. The button will popup a dialog where brushes can be selected and each of the characteristics of the brush can be modified. SF-BRUSH "Brush" '("Circle (03)" 100 44 0) Here the brush dialog will be popped up with a default brush of Circle (03) opacity 100 spacing 44 and paint mode of Normal (value 0). If this selection was unchanged the value passed to the function as a parameter would be '("Circle (03)" 100 44 0).
SF-PATTERN	It will create a widget in the control dialog. The widget consists of a preview area (which when pressed will produce a popup preview) and a button with the "..." label. The button will popup a dialog where patterns can be selected. SF-PATTERN "Pattern" "Maple Leaves" The value returned when the script is invoked is a string containing the pattern name. If the above selection was not altered the string would contain "Maple Leaves".
SF-GRADIENT	It will create a widget in the control dialog. The widget consists of a button containing a preview of the selected gradient.

279

	If the button is pressed a gradient selection dialog will popup. SF-GRADIENT "Gradient" "Deep Sea" The value returned when the script is invoked is a string containing the gradient name. If the above selection was not altered the string would contain "Deep Sea".
SF-PALETTE	It will create a widget in the control dialog. The widget consists of a button containing the name of the selected palette. If the button is pressed a palette selection dialog will popup. SF-PALETTE "Palette" "Named Colors" The value returned when the script is invoked is a string containing the palette name. If the above selection was not altered the string would contain "Named Colors".
SF-FILENAME	It will create a widget in the control dialog. The widget consists of a button containing the name of a file. If the button is pressed a file selection dialog will popup. SF-FILENAME "label" (string-append "" gimp-data-directory "/scripts/beavis.jpg") The value returned when the script is invoked is a string containing the filename.
SF-DIRNAME	Only useful in interactive mode. Very similar to SF-FILENAME, but the created widget allows to choose a directory instead of a file. SF-DIRNAME "label" "/var/tmp/images" The value returned when the script is invoked is a string containing the dirname.

SF-OPTION	It will create a widget in the control dialog. The widget is a combo-box showing the options that are passed as a list. The first option is the default choice. SF-OPTION "label" '("option1" "option2") The value returned when the script is invoked is the number of the chosen option, where the option first is counted as 0.
SF-ENUM	It will create a widget in the control dialog. The widget is a combo-box showing all enum values for the given enum type. This has to be the name of a registered enum, without the "Gimp" prefix. The second parameter speficies the default value, using the enum value's nick. SF-ENUM "Interpolation" '("InterpolationType" "linear") The value returned when the script is invoked corresponds to chosen enum value.

Before version 2.6, <Toolbox> could be also used, but now the toolbox menu is removed, so don't use it.

The original, written by Mike, says put the menu entry in the Script-Fu menu of the Xtns menu at the Toolbox, but since version 2.6, the Toolbox menu had been removed and merged with the image window menubar.

This section is not part of the original tutorial.

3.5. Giving Our Script Some Guts

Let us continue with our training and add some functionality to our script.

3.5.1. Creating A New Image

In the previous lesson, we created an empty function and registered it with GIMP. In this lesson, we want to provide functionality to our script — we want to create a new image, add the user's text to it and resize the image to fit the text exactly.

Once you know how to set variables, define functions and access list members, the rest is all downhill — all you need to do is familiarize yourself with the functions available in GIMP's procedural database and call those functions directly. So fire up the **Section 12.7, "The Procedure Browser"** and let's get cookin'!

Let's begin by making a new image. We'll create a new variable, theImage, set to the result of calling GIMP's built-in function gimp-image-new.

As you can see from the DB Browser, the function gimp-image-new takes three parameters — the image's width, height and the type of image. Because we'll later resize the image to fit the text, we'll make a 10x10 pixels RGB image. We'll store the image's width and sizes in some variables, too, as we'll refer to and manipulate them later in the script.

```
(define (script-fu-text-box inText inFont inFontSize inTextColor)
(let*
    (
      ; define our local variables
      ; create a new image:
      (theImageWidth  10)
      (theImageHeight 10)
      (theImage (car
                  (gimp-image-new
                    theImageWidth
                    theImageHeight
                    RGB
                  )
                )
      )
      (theText)     ;a declaration for the text
                    ;we create later
```

Note: We used the value RGB to specify that the image is an RGB image. We could have also used 0, but RGB is more descriptive when we glance at the code.

You should also notice that we took the head of the result of the function call. This may seem strange, because the database explicitly tells us that it returns only one value — the ID of the newly created image. However, all GIMP functions return a list, even if there is only one element in the list, so we need to get the head of the list.

3.5.2. Adding A New Layer To The Image

Now that we have an image, we need to add a layer to it. We'll call the gimp-layer-new function to create the layer, passing in the ID of the image we just created. (From now on, instead of listing the complete function, we'll only list the lines we're adding to it. You can see the complete script here.) Because we've declared all of the local variables we'll use, we'll also close the parentheses marking the end of our variable declarations:

```
;create a new layer for the image:
  (theLayer
        (car
            (gimp-layer-new
             theImage
             theImageWidth
             theImageHeight
             RGB-IMAGE
             "layer 1"
             100
             NORMAL
            )
        )
  )
) ;end of our local variables
```

Once we have the new layer, we need to add it to the image:

```
(gimp-image-add-layer theImage theLayer 0)
```

Now, just for fun, let's see the fruits of our labors up until this point, and add this line to show the new, empty image:

(gimp-display-new theImage)

Save your work, select Filters → Script-Fu → Refresh Scripts, run the script and a new image should pop up. It will probably contain garbage (random colors), because we haven't erased it. We'll get to that in a second.

3.5.3. Adding The Text

Go ahead and remove the line to display the image (or comment it out with a (;) as the first character of the line).

Before we add text to the image, we need to set the background and foreground colors so that the text appears in the color the user specified. We'll use the gimp-context-set-back/foreground functions:

```
(gimp-context-set-background '(255 255 255) )
(gimp-context-set-foreground inTextColor)
```

With the colors properly set, let's now clean out the garbage currently in the image by filling the drawable with the background color:

```
(gimp-drawable-fill theLayer BACKGROUND-FILL)
```

With the image cleared, we're ready to add some text:

```
(set! theText
      (car
          (gimp-text-fontname
           theImage theLayer
           0 0
           inText
           0
           TRUE
           inFontSize PIXELS
           "Sans")
      )
)
```

Although a long function call, it's fairly straightforward if you go over the parameters while looking at the function's entry in the DB Browser. Basically, we're creating a new text layer and assigning it to the variable theText.

Now that we have the text, we can grab its width and height and resize the image and the image's layer to the text's size:

```
(set! theImageWidth   (car (gimp-drawable-width  theText) ) )
(set! theImageHeight  (car (gimp-drawable-height theText) ) )

(gimp-image-resize theImage theImageWidth theImageHeight 0 0)

(gimp-layer-resize theLayer theImageWidth theImageHeight 0 0)
```

If you're like me, you're probably wondering what a drawable is when compared to a layer. The difference between the two is that a drawable is anything that can be drawn into, including layers but also channels, layer masks, the selection, etc; a layer is a more specific version of a drawable. In most cases, the distinction is not important.

With the image ready to go, we can now re-add our display line:

```
(gimp-display-new theImage)
```

Save your work, refresh the database and give your first script a run!

3.5.4. Clearing The Dirty Flag

If you try to close the image created without first saving the file, GIMP will ask you if you want to save your work before you close the image. It asks this because the image is marked as dirty, or unsaved. In the case of our script, this is a nuisance for the times when we simply give it a test run and don't add or change anything in the resulting image — that is, our work is easily reproducible in such a simple script, so it makes sense to get rid of this dirty flag.

To do this, we can clear the dirty flag after displaying the image:

    (gimp-image-clean-all theImage)

This will set dirty count to 0, making it appear to be a "clean" image.

Whether to add this line or not is a matter of personal taste. I use it in scripts that produce new images, where the results are trivial, as in this case. If your script is very complicated, or if it works on an existing image, you will probably not want to use this function.

3.6. Extending The Text Box Script
3.6.1. Handling Undo Correctly

When creating a script, you want to give your users the ability to undo their actions, should they make a mistake. This is easily accomplished by calling the functions gimp-undo-push-group-start and gimp-undo-push-group-end around the code that manipulates the image. You can think of them as matched statements that let GIMP know when to start and stop recording manipulations on the image, so that those manipulations can later be undone.

If you are creating a new image entirely, it doesn't make sense to use these functions because you're not changing an existing image. However, when you are changing an existing image, you most surely want to use these functions.

Undoing a script works nearly flawlessly when using these functions.

3.6.2. Extending The Script A Little More

Now that we have a very handy-dandy script to create text boxes, let's add two features to it:

- Currently, the image is resized to fit exactly around the text — there's no room for anything, like drop shadows or special effects (even

though many scripts will automatically resize the image as necessary). Let's add a buffer around the text, and even let the user specify how much buffer to add as a percentage of the size of the resultant text.
- This script could easily be used in other scripts that work with text. Let's extend it so that it returns the image and the layers, so other scripts can call this script and use the image and layers we create.

3.6.3. Modifying The Parameters And The Registration Function

To let the user specify the amount of buffer, we'll add a parameter to our function and the registration function:

```
(define (script-fu-text-box inTest inFont inFontSize inTextColor inBufferAmount)
(let*
    (
      ; define our local variables
      ; create a new image:
      (theImageWidth  10)
      (theImageHeight 10)
      (theImage (car
                  (gimp-image-new
                    theImageWidth
                    theImageHeight
                    RGB
                  )
              )
      )
      (theText)        ;a declaration for the text
                       ;we create later

      (theBuffer)      ;added

      (theLayer
              (car
                (gimp-layer-new
                  theImage
                  theImageWidth
                  theImageHeight
                  RGB-IMAGE
                  "layer 1"
                  100
                  NORMAL
                )
              )
      )
    ) ;end of our local variables

  [Code here]
)

(script-fu-register
  "script-fu-text-box"           ;func name
  "Text Box"                     ;menu label
```

```
    "Creates a simple text box, sized to fit\
      around the user's choice of text,\
      font, font size, and color."           ;description
    "Michael Terry"                          ;author
    "copyright 1997, Michael Terry;\
      2009, the GIMP Documentation Team"     ;copyright notice
    "October 27, 1997"                       ;date created
    ""                    ;image type that the script works on
    SF-STRING     "Text"       "Text Box"  ;a string variable
    SF-FONT       "Font"       "Charter"   ;a font variable
    SF-ADJUSTMENT "Font size"  '(50 1 1000 1 10 0 1)
                                            ;a spin-button
    SF-COLOR      "Color"      '(0 0 0)    ;color variable
    SF-ADJUSTMENT "Buffer amount" '(35 0 100 1 10 1 0)
                                            ;a slider
  )
  (script-fu-menu-register "script-fu-text-box" "<Image>/Font/Create/Text")
```

3.6.4. Adding The New Code

We're going to add code in two places: right before we resize the image, and at the end of the script (to return the new image, the layer and the text).

After we get the text's height and width, we need to resize these values based on the buffer amount specified by the user. We won't do any error checking to make sure it's in the range of 0-100% because it's not life-threatening, and because there's no reason why the user can't enter a value like "200" as the percent of buffer to add.

```
    (set! theBuffer (* theImageHeight (/ inBufferAmount 100) ) )

    (set! theImageHeight (+ theImageHeight theBuffer theBuffer) )
    (set! theImageWidth  (+ theImageWidth  theBuffer theBuffer) )
```

All we're doing here is setting the buffer based on the height of the text, and adding it twice to both the height and width of our new image. (We add it twice to both dimensions because the buffer needs to be added to both sides of the text.)

Now that we have resized the image to allow for a buffer, we need to center the text within the image. This is done by moving it to the (x, y) coordinates of (theBuffer, theBuffer). I added this line after resizing the layer and the image:

```
    (gimp-layer-set-offsets theText theBuffer theBuffer)
```

Go ahead and save your script, and try it out after refreshing the database.

All that is left to do is return our image, the layer, and the text layer. After displaying the image, we add this line:

(list theImage theLayer theText)

This is the last line of the function, making this list available to other scripts that want to use it.

To use our new text box script in another script, we could write something like the following:

```
(set! theResult (script-fu-text-box
          "Some text"
          "Charter" "30"
          '(0 0 0)
          "35"
          )
)
(gimp-image-flatten (car theResult))
```

Congratulations, you are on your way to your Black Belt of Script-Fu!

3.7. Your script and its working
3.7.1. What you write

Below the complete script:

```
(script-fu-register
     "script-fu-text-box"              ;func name
     "Text Box"                        ;menu label
     "Creates a simple text box, sized to fit\
       around the user's choice of text,\
       font, font size, and color."    ;description
     "Michael Terry"                   ;author
     "copyright 1997, Michael Terry;\
      2009, the GIMP Documentation Team"   ;copyright notice
     "October 27, 1997"                ;date created
     ""                 ;image type that the script works on
     SF-STRING     "Text"      "Text Box"  ;a string variable
     SF-FONT       "Font"      "Charter"   ;a font variable
     SF-ADJUSTMENT "Font size"  '(50 1 1000 1 10 0 1)
                                ;a spin-button
     SF-COLOR      "Color"     '(0 0 0)   ;color variable
     SF-ADJUSTMENT "Buffer amount" '(35 0 100 1 10 1 0)
                     ;a slider
)
(script-fu-menu-register "script-fu-text-box" "<Image>/File/Create/Text")
(define (script-fu-text-box inText inFont inFontSize inTextColor inBufferAmount)
  (let*
```

```
(
  ; define our local variables
  ; create a new image:
  (theImageWidth  10)
  (theImageHeight 10)
  (theImage)
  (theImage
     (car
        (gimp-image-new
          theImageWidth
          theImageHeight
          RGB
        )
     )
  )
  (theText)          ;a declaration for the text
  (theBuffer)        ;create a new layer for the image
  (theLayer
     (car
        (gimp-layer-new
          theImage
          theImageWidth
          theImageHeight
          RGB-IMAGE
          "layer 1"
          100
          NORMAL
        )
     )
  )
) ;end of our local variables
(gimp-image-add-layer theImage theLayer 0)
(gimp-context-set-background '(255 255 255) )
(gimp-context-set-foreground inTextColor)
(gimp-drawable-fill theLayer BACKGROUND-FILL)
(set! theText
       (car
          (gimp-text-fontname
            theImage theLayer
            0 0
            inText
            0
            TRUE
            inFontSize PIXELS
            "Sans")
       )
)
(set! theImageWidth   (car (gimp-drawable-width  theText) ) )
(set! theImageHeight  (car (gimp-drawable-height theText) ) )
(set! theBuffer (* theImageHeight (/ inBufferAmount 100) ) )
(set! theImageHeight (+ theImageHeight theBuffer theBuffer) )
(set! theImageWidth  (+ theImageWidth  theBuffer theBuffer) )
(gimp-image-resize theImage theImageWidth theImageHeight 0 0)
(gimp-layer-resize theLayer theImageWidth theImageHeight 0 0)
(gimp-layer-set-offsets theText theBuffer theBuffer)
```

```
    (gimp-display-new theImage)
    (list theImage theLayer theText)
  )
)
```

3.7.2. What you obtain

Figure 13.5. And the result on the screen.

Appendix

1. The Very Beginning

According to Peter Mattis and Spencer Kimball, the original creators of GIMP, in their announcement of GIMP 0.54:

The GIMP arose from the ashes of a hideously crafted CS164 (compilers) class project. The setting: early morning. We were both weary from lack of sleep and the terrible strain of programming a compiler in LISP. The limits of our patience had long been exceeded, and yet still the dam held.

And then it happened. Common LISP messily dumped core when it could not allocate the 17 MB it needed to generate a parser for a simple grammar using yacc. An unbelieving moment passed, there was one shared look of disgust, and then our project was vapor. We had to write something... *ANYTHING* ... useful. Something in C. Something that did not rely on nested lists to represent a bitmap. Thus, the GIMP was born.

Like the phoenix, glorious, new life sprung out of the burnt remnants of LISP and yacc. Ideas went flying, decisions were made, the GIMP began to take form.

An image manipulation program was the consensus. A program that would at the very least lessen the necessity of using commercial software under "Windoze" or on the "Macintoy". A program that would provide the features missing from the other X painting and imaging tools. A program that would help maintain the long tradition of excellent and free UNIX applications.

Six months later, we've reached an early beta stage. We want to release now to start working on compatibility issues and cross-platform stability. Also, we feel now that the program is actually usable and would like to see other interested programmers developing plug-ins and various file format support.

2. The Early Days of GIMP

Version 0.54

> Version 0.54 was released in February 1996, and had a major impact as the first truly professional free image manipulation program. This was the first free program that could compete with the big commercial image manipulation programs.
>
> Version 0.54 was a beta release, but it was so stable that you could use it for daily work. However, one of the major drawbacks of 0.54 was that the toolkit (the slidebars, menus, dialog boxes, etc.) was built on Motif, a commercial toolkit. This was a big drawback for systems like "Linux", because you had to buy Motif if you wanted to use the faster, dynamically linked GIMP. Many developers were also students running Linux, who could not afford to buy Motif.

Version 0.60

> When 0.60 was released in July 1996, it had been under S and P (Spencer and Peter) development for four months. Main programming advantages were the new toolkits, GTK (GIMP Toolkit) and gdk (GIMP Drawing Kit), which eliminated the reliance on Motif. For the graphic artist, 0.60 was full of new features like: basic layers; improved painting tools (sub-pixel sampling, brush spacing); a better airbrush; paint modes; etc.
>
> Version 0.60 was only a developer's release, and was not intended for widespread use. It served as a workbench for 0.99 and the final 1.0 version, so functions and enhancement could be tested and dropped or changed. You can look at 0.60 as the alpha version of 0.99.

Version 0.99

> In February 1997, 0.99 came on the scene. Together with other developers, S and P had made several changes to GIMP and added even more features. The main difference was the new API (Application Programming Interface) and the "PDB", which made it possible to write scripts; Script-Fus (or macros) could now automate things that you would normally do by hand. GTK/gdk had also changed and was now called GTK+. In addition, 0.99 used a new form of tile-based memory handling that made it possible to load huge images into GIMP

(loading a 100 MB image into GIMP is no problem). Version 0.99 also introduced a new native GIMP file format called XCF.

The new API made it really easy to write extensions and plug-ins for GIMP. Several new plug-ins and extensions emerged to make GIMP even more useful (such as SANE, which enables scanning directly into GIMP).

In the summer of 1997, GIMP had reached version 0.99.10, and S and P had to drop most of their support since they had graduated and begun jobs. However, the other developers of GIMP continued under the orchestration of Federico Mena to make GIMP ready for prime time.

GTK+ was separated from GIMP in September 1997. GTK+ had been recognized as an excellent toolkit, and other developers began using it to build their own applications.

GIMP went into feature freeze in October 1997. This meant that no new features would be added to the GIMP core libraries and program. GUM (GIMP Users Manual) version 0.5 was also released early in October 1997. The developing work continued to make GIMP stable and ready for version 1.0.

How to Receive Your Part III (Three) PDF Copy

This is the "**You Don't Have to Pay for Part III Section**"

Part III (three) explains Function Reference in a detailed form using fully colored images, its chapters include: **Chapter14: Tools, Chapter 15: Dialogs, Chapter 16: Menus and Chapter 17: Filters.** The above listed chapters have sections and sub sections all treated in a detailed way. A great way of knowing more about GIMP 2.8.

It is an important part of this GIMP book especially for those who are not yet professionals in GIMP or those who want to know more about it.

Why was part three not included in the main book?

We initially included Part Three in the main book but it caused the list price of the book to become terribly expensive due to images included in it, we think that will make its demand low and may eventually turn most customers away, thereby making us not to achieve our aim for this book. When we talk about Part three, we are talking about a part of this book that has about a thousand pages in a different book. Like we said earlier, this book is to help people use GIMP better and not to extort money from our customers in any way.

Eligibility: Any customer who purchases this book (Brighter Days with GIMP) is automatically eligible for the full colour PDF file of Part Three irrespective of the customer's location or purchase time.

How to Get Your Part Three Copy.

- Buy a copy of Brighter Days with GIMP
- Write a review (optional)
  Note: In as much as this is not compulsory, we want you to know that it helps to make the verification of your purchase of the main book (Brighter Days with GIMP) faster.
- Send a mail to **contactucabelbooks@gmail**.com
  Once we receive your mail, we will send the Part Three PDF copy via the email address you used to contact us.

Part III starts from **Chapter 14** of the PDF file that you will receive.

Thanks for your patronage.